Southern Italian Home Cooking

Southern Italian Home Cooking

FRANK AND DOMINIC CRINITI

NEW HOLLAND

Sharing food with family and friends is sacred and should be cherished. We would like to thank our grandparents Nonna Raffaela Pelli and in memory of Nonno Domenico Pelli, Nonno Francesco Criniti and Nonna Caterina Criniti.

We would also like to thank our parents Cosimo and Rosa Criniti, sisters Kathy and Raffaela and other relatives and friends who have helped create and share our passion for southern Italian cuisine.

Contents

Summer

Autumn

Winter

My Southern Italian Childhood
Frank Criniti

When I was young I dreamt of being a cowboy.
When I worked out that wasn't actually a job,
I fell in love with pizza.
My Papá used to take us to a pizza shop and on
every visit, there was a brown-eyed brunette girl
around my age standing out the front of the shop
who would hand me a rose.
I had a crush on this girl – but I loved to go there
because the pizza was so good. I would stand at
the window watching the man making this doughy
delight and it was from this point I knew this was
something I wanted to do. When I finally decided
to pursue my dream of owning a pizza shop, I
travelled to Italy, going from region to region.
In Calabria, where my family is from, I watched
the casareca (a curling, twisting pasta perfect
for catching and holding sauces) being rolled. I
collected menus and cookbooks. Food became an
obsession. I wanted everyone to know what it was
like to taste proper, authentic southern Italian food.
Having enjoyed it so much growing up, I felt it was
only fair to pass it on.

Every night at dinner our family table was set as though for a party of a hundred.

At first glance one would assume that we were expecting other guests to arrive. To an outsider, a Calabrian table could appear to have been strategically prepared in such a way to conceal the table cloth. Making room for your own plate on the table was the first challenge, choosing where to start from was another as you had to make sure you didn't fill up on antipasto and leave room for the rest of the food to follow.

There were dishes we could almost guarantee to find regularly on our table from produce available all year round. But it was summer that made all the difference because fresh fennel, artichokes and garden grown broccoli was on offer.

Seating positions on our table were never debated. Papá would always sit at the head of the table, with Ma sitting to his left and I was always to his right. My brother Dom and sisters Kathy and Raffaela also had their set places. As we sat savouring the staple Calabrese dishes of Pepperonata, Briscoli de riso and the Pana Duro that we'd soak into a tomato salad until it absorbed all the oils and juices running down our forearms, we were doing more than just eating, we were connecting. Papá would talk about his latest visit to the markets, Ma would share the latest healing remedies using parsley, my siblings and I would be in stitches reminiscing over the time that firecrackers blew up all over Papá's salamis. The joy came from the fact that we were never told to quieten down no matter how loud our laughs got, or how high our voices went; my parents knew that meal time was the only time of the day we could exchange stories as a family.

Since Papá wasn't the overly expressive type, there was something about sitting at the table that revealed his true affections toward us. Whether it be sharing the glass of wine that he'd retrieved from the cellar with Ma, or sneakily adding a drop of the wine into our lemonades because it was healing, the dinner table was a place of love. I now imagine that as Papá sat there at the head of the table watching his four children devouring the fresh breads, the antipasto, sauces, the pastas and fresh salads, he would have been feeling a great sense of pride and gratitude for his southern Italian heritage. It was this food that united the people before him. For food to have that power of connecting is a truly marvellous thing.

Basic Recipes

~

Our Ma's Kitchen
Frank Criniti

Ma's old-style kitchen had a granite bench
top, old timber cabinets and marble floor
and on the bench, near the stove, sat an old
terracotta oil bottle and next to that, a wine
bottle in an old bamboo casing.
The sound of the stove fan could be heard, as
well as the clinkering of the hung pots and
pans.
My earliest childhood memories are of
waking up on Sunday mornings to the
banging of pots and pans, the smell of
simmering garlic, olive oil, fresh tomatoes
and Ma in the kitchen preparing her famous
sugo di pomodoro, spaghetti and meatballs.
The aroma of the sauce throughout the house
was so mouth-watering that when Ma wasn't
looking we would sneak pieces of bread and
dip it into the pot of sauce.
Ma would usually turn a blind eye but by the
fifth dip she would call out 'Non rovinare l
appetito! (Don't ruin your appetite!).
We have always loved both food and the

process of creating a meal; all the way from its preparation to its consumption. Ma always had a bowl of freshly cut fruit that was always on the kitchen bench, the lentil soup that Nonna (grandmother) would have Nonno (grandfather) deliver to our doorstep, and the antipasto platter that had its permanent place on our dinner table. When I eat, I examine, I explore. I am lost in thought, looking at the plate in front of me and then I drift off into space as I take my first bite. I want to taste every flavor, smell every aroma, and as I do so, my eyes come alive with complete enjoyment and satisfaction.

In every Italian kitchen there are staples – tomato sauce, olives, crusty bread, cured meat and of course, pasta. Here are a few basic recipes that can be used in many of the dishes in Southern Italian Homecooking. Have these on hand, and you have a meal.

Salsa Pomodoro

BASIC TOMATO SAUCE

PREPARATION TIME: 30 MINUTES

4kg (8½lbs) tomatoes
  (fresh from the markets—buy per box if
  you can)

fresh basil leaves
10 x 750ml (1 pint) glass bottles,
  or old beer bottles

Prepare the bottles

Clean the bottles with a brush and hot water, 2-3 times. Leave them upside down to drip dry. Make sure they are completely dry before filling them.

Prepare the tomatoes

Clean the tomatoes under cool water to remove any chemicals and remove their green stems. Slice them in quarters and crush them by hand with a masher or with a machine. The tomato sauce will now be separated from the seeds and the skin. Discard the seeds using a course sieve (they can be used as compost).

Fill the bottles

Using a funnel, fill the bottles with the tomato mixture. Add 2 fresh basil leaves per bottle then tightly seal with beer cap or screw top lid.

Cooking and storage

The bottles then need to be boiled. You can do this individually on your stove top or if you are cooking on mass use a gallon drum with a gas burner underneath.

Place each bottle down flat and cover with warm water and boil quickly for 20-30 minutes.

Turn off the heat and allow the bottles to sit in the water until it cools, usually until the next day.

Remove the bottles and store them in a cool place, such as a garage, cellar or other location away from the sun.

This sauce will keep for up to two years.

Tip

You can also make a larger quantity than this. For 20kg of tomatoes you will be able to make 50 bottles of sauce.

Our father had a habit of adding extra olive oil which explains my love of the fresh taste of oil. If you are feeling adventurous, add an extra dash of extra virgin olive oil... for Papà!

Sugo di Pomodoro Fresco

NAPOLITANA TOMATO SAUCE

PREPARATION TIME: *20 MINUTES*

COOKING TIME: *1 HOUR AND 15 MINUTES*

MAKES: *400ML (16½ FL OZ)*

60ml (2 fl oz) extra virgin olive oil
2 cloves garlic, thinly sliced
425g (15oz) can peeled crushed tomatoes or 6 fresh tomatoes, cooked, peeled and crushed

1 teaspoon sugar
salt and pepper
5 fresh basil leaves, torn

In a pan, heat oil and garlic until garlic is lightly golden, then add crushed peeled tomatoes and stir. Bring to a boil and let simmer. Add sugar, salt and pepper and simmer until sauce has reduced by one quarter. Finish with basil leaves and stir them through the sauce.

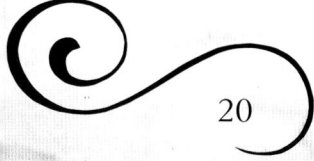

This simple dish has been adopted across the world and everyone seems to have their own take on Bolognese. Here is the best Bolognese recipe to take you to the rustic southern Italian place our family called home.

Bolognaise Ragù

BOLOGNAISE SAUCE

PREPARATION TIME: *30 MINUTES*

COOKING TIME: *1½-2 HOURS*

SERVES: *6*

10 ripe Roma tomatoes

½ cup olive oil

1 onion, diced

2 garlic cloves, crushed and chopped

1 birdseye chilli, sliced (optional)

150g (5¼ oz) lean beef mince

1 veal or pork chop

¼ cup red wine

1 teaspoon sugar

sprinkle of dried oregano

4 basil leaves

1 bay leaf

1 cup water

salt and pepper

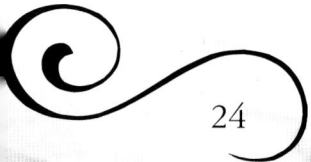

Bring a large pot of water to the boil. Using a sharp knife, make a cross on the top of the tomatoes and place them in the boiling water and cook for around 10 minutes. When cooked and soft, drain tomatoes and set aside to cool. When cooled, peel off the skin beginning at the cross marked on the tops. Place tomatoes into a blender and give them a quick blitz. (We have a great Italian contraption for this called a 'macchina pomodoro' which was used before the invention of the blender and my mother uses this still today. She has never used a blender.) Set pulped tomato to one side.

Heat oil in a large heavy based pot to medium heat and add onion, garlic and chilli if using. Stir this until the aroma of the garlic has made its way to your nose. Add the minced meat and fry gently, releasing the flavours. Add the veal chop and brown slightly. Then add the pureed tomatoes, wine and half the quantity of water. Combine well. Bring to boil for 8 to 10 minutes, which allows the alcohol in the wine to cook off as you don't want it to dominate the sauce.

Reduce heat to low and cook sauce for around an hour and a half, stirring every 20 minutes and gradually adding remaining water with each stir. Add sugar (to neutralise the acid in the tomatoes), season with salt and pepper and a sprinkling of oregano. Ten minutes before the end of cooking, add the bay leaf as it will release a little bit more love into the sauce. Stir ragú through your favourite pasta, sprinkle with parmesan and serve.

Tip

Stirring the sauce while it's simmering will prevent it from becoming bitter. Cook your pasta al dente, as this will complement the dish more than words can express and I personally only use spaghetti or a very thin linguini. Don't forget to use good quality parmesan cheese...my mouth is watering already!

Bechamel Sauce

White sauce

Preparation time: 10 minutes

Cooking time: 20 minutes

Makes: 1.4L

100g (3½ oz) unsalted butter

100g (3½ oz) plain flour
  (all-purpose flour)

1L (2 pints) milk

nutmeg, pinch

salt, pinch

white pepper, pinch

Place butter and plain flour in a pot and stir continously on a medium to high heat, until it forms a paste. Add half of the milk and stir vigorously until it blends smoothly with the flour. Gradually add remainder of the milk and nutmeg, stirring until it thickens. Finish by adding salt and pepper.

Zia (aunt) Sapenza arrived one morning at about 10am at Zio (uncle) Bruno's house in Catanzaro and to our delight she announced she was making lunch. We were then told that she had a knack for making fresh pasta, it was her specialty. So she asked us to join her outside.

She proceeded to a large tree in my uncle's backyard and then ripped a long twig off one of the extended branches. she cleaned it and took a closer look. She looked as though she would discipline us with it!

That was not her intention, her reason for selecting this perfect piece of wood was to make her famous long fresh spaghetti. She made her fresh pasta and told us stories as it rested.

Then when she was ready to roll it out she asked Frank to film her so she could send a message to our father via the video recorder, while she cut and rolled and twigged her famous spaghetti with this ever most rustic, organic tool we had ever seen being used for food. By twirling pasta around the twig, the pasta took on a curly shape.

You can also use a verga (rod) or knitting needle.

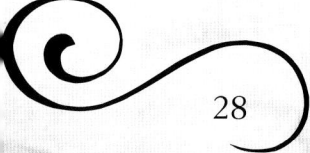

Fresh Pasta

Preparation time: 25 minutes

Cooking time: 10 minutes

Makes: 350g (1¾ oz) (12 ⅓ oz) fresh pasta

200g (7oz) unbleached flour   cold water to sprinkle

1 whole egg plus 1 egg yolk   olive oil

Using a clean benchtop, place the flour in a heap and make a well in the centre. Place egg in the centre and work flour into the eggs. Once it is combined, sprinkle with cold water as you work and knead your dough. This should help to loosen it a little.

Knead for 8 minutes until the dough is smooth to touch and elastic.

Allow to rest for 30 minutes wrapped in a tea towel. Your dough is now ready to use for tortellini, ravioli or long pasta.

Spring

~

Breakfast
Veal baked with eggs and cheese

Starter
Fried bread

Fried mozzarella with
* spicy tomato sauce*

Frittata

Marinated beef

Grilled quail

Side
Mozzarella and tomato
* salad*

Spaghetti with clams

Pasta and goat sauce

Pasta with chickpeas

Main Course
Stuffed veal rolls

Chicken in tomato sauce

Seafood in white wine

Breaded veal cutlet

Sweet
Cannoli

Tiramisu

Baking
Lemon biscuits with
* lemon icing*

Calabrese Easter Cake

Italian Life
Frank Criniti

I travelled to Italy for the first time when I was 21. Having never set foot in my native homeland, I was in the safe company and under the guidance of my sister Raffaela and Ma, Rosa.

Arriving in Rome, I was surprised to learn that nobody could understand the Italian I was speaking! I was certain that my parents brought me up speaking Italian at home. Apparently the Calabrian dialect is not easily understood by people from outside Calabria.

It was the Italian summer when we finally reached Santa Caterina after a long bus journey through the patchwork splendour of the Calabrian countryside.

Located on the tip of the Italian 'boot', in the extreme south of Italy, Santa Caterina is lapped by the splendid crystal blue Ionian and Tyrrhenian Seas. The town is so small that it has only one light post, a wooden bench, and a small fountain in the centre of the square. Despite its size, there was something about that town that seemed to envelope my heart.

My Zio (uncle) Bruno and Zia (aunt) Rosa's home smelt familiar and their kitchen table resembled that of our own. The memory is still vivid in my mind of a basket stuffed with large heads of fresh fennel and just picked vegetables. There certainly was no mistaking southern hospitality either, as my Zia Sapienza was concerned that we all looked frail and suffering from malnutrition.

So began my passion with the way of the south, my trip back to my parents' villages in the southern most tip of Italy gave everything meaning. From that trip I felt a great sense of achievement and as though my life had been given true meaning – to live, learn and share the great experiences of my ancestors through the love of food. I was drenched in the culture and bursting with excitement to re discover the colours of my own home garden growing up and the way fresh, seasonal produce dictated the dinner table.

Our Grandfather's Garden

In Nonno (grandfather) Dominic's garden, which always smelt like burnt timber and cardboard, sat a vegetable patch organised by slabs of concrete. As children, we were only ever allowed to walk on these concrete slabs to avoid trampling the precious vegies. We had our own little vegetable patch at home but it was no competition for my Nonno's. He grew parsley, spinach, tomatoes, chillies, corn, Italian Roma beans, and lettuce. The image of the string line set up from his veranda to his fig tree has stuck in my mind; he'd tug on the string every so often to scare the birds from eating his figs. It is from this garden that we developed our appreciation and passion for fresh produce.

*Nonno Pelli and
Zio Frank Pelli in
the Provincia Di
Catanzavo, Arena,
Calabria.*

*Italians use food as a way of showing love and
affection. Papá always said that words unspoken
are the best words said, a mantra that we live
by today. To Italians, the simple act of making
someone a meal, or sharing their produce,
speaks volumes.
Our Nonno maintained his vegie
patch everyday until his death,
aged 79. That little corner of
the earth provided our family
with some of the most organic,
nurtured, and loved produce that
we had ever eaten.*

*Our sister Kathy in
Papá Cosimo's garden.*

This traditional breakfast dish is perfect for a weekend morning or light lunch.

Carne Pizziaolo con Uovo

VEAL BAKED WITH EGGS AND CHEESE

PREPARATION TIME: 45 MINUTES

COOKING TIME: 35 MINUTES

SERVES: 4

800g (28oz) veal fillet (thin schnitzel)

200g (7oz) plain flour (all-purpose flour)

160ml (2 fl oz) extra virgin olive oil

3 cloves garlic, sliced

1 small Spanish (purple) onion

800ml (1½ pints) Napolitana Tomato
   Sauce (see Basic Recipes)

½ cup water

3 fresh basil leaves, chopped

12 eggs

pinch of dried oregano

salt and pepper

pane di casa or other crusty white bread,
   and provolone or parmesan to serve

Tenderise the veal with a meat mallet and season and dust in plain flour. Heat half the olive oil in a large pot, and fry veal until golden on each side. Remove veal from pan and set aside to rest on absorbent paper.

In the same pan add remaining oil and allow to heat, add sliced garlic and onion, fry for approximately 2 minutes on medium heat, then add Napolitana Tomato Sauce.

Simmer for 10 minutes, return cooked veal plus any juices to the sauce. Add water and stir through. Season to taste, sprinkle with oregano and fresh basil.

Crack 3 eggs on top of the sauce. Cover pan with a lid and simmer for 2 to 3 minutes. Top with shaved provolone or parmigana cheese to serve. Enjoy with toasted pane di casa or crusty white bread.

Pane in Carozza

FRIED BREAD

PREPARATION TIME: 35 MINUTES PLUS CHILLING

COOKING TIME: 25 MINUTES

SERVES: 4

8 slices, thickly sliced white bread

350g (12$^{1/3}$ oz) Cheese Sauce
  (see Basic Recipes)

200g (7oz) plain flour
  (all-purpose flour)

6 eggs

120ml (4fl oz) milk

400g (14oz) breadcrumbs

pinch dried oregano

salt and pepper

1.5L (3 pints) cottonseed oil

Cut the crust from the bread, spread béchamel sauce on one slice then place the two slices together to make a sandwich and dust with flour. In a large bowl, mix egg and milk to make a batter and season with salt and pepper.

Dip each sandwich into the batter and soak until they drip slightly, then roll in breadcrumb and oregano mixture until completely covered. After all sandwiches are coated with batter and crumb, dip each again in batter and crumb, so all are double coated. Place on a plate, cover with cling film and refrigerate until set, about 3 hours. In a frying pan, heat cottonseed oil to 180°C/350°F until breadcrumbs become golden brown. Season with salt.

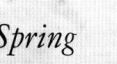

Mozzarella Fritta con Pomodora Piccannte

FRIED MOZZARELLA WITH SPICY TOMATO SAUCE

PREPARATION TIME: *45 MINUTES PLUS CHILLING*

COOKING TIME: *45 MINUTES*

SERVES: *4*

1kg (2lbs) (2lbs) buffalo mozzarella cheese

150g (5¼ oz) plain flour
   (all-purpose flour)

4 eggs, lightly beaten

50ml (1½ fl oz) milk

salt and pepper

250g (9oz) breadcrumbs

pinch dried oregano

2L (4 pints) cottonseed oil

SAUCE

40ml (1^1/$_3$ fl oz) extra virgin olive oil

2 garlic cloves, thinly sliced

2 whole birdseye chilli, thinly sliced

500ml (1 pint) Napolitana Tomato Sauce
   (see Basic Recipes)

6 basil leaves, torn

salt and pepper

Cut buffalo mozzarella into bite-sized pieces and lightly coat in flour.

Beat eggs, milk, salt and pepper to make a batter and dip dusted mozzarella into the batter, then dip into a mixture of breadcrumb and oregano.

Repeat process so cheese has been double-crumbed. Place on a plate, cover in cling film and refrigerate until set, about 2 hours.

Meanwhile, make spicy tomato sauce. Heat oil and garlic and cook until garlic starts to colour. Add chilli and Napolitana Sauce, reduce to thick consistency. Set aside.

To cook mozzarella balls, heat cottonseed oil to 180°C/350°F and fry until golden. Serve with warm spicy tomato sauce.

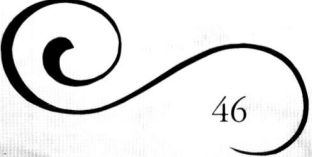

Frittata

ITALIAN OMELETTE

PREPARATION TIME: 15 MINUTES

COOKING TIME: 20 MINUTES

SERVES: 6

8 eggs
½ cup mozzarella or
other soft Italian cheese
2 zucchini (courgette)
salt and pepper

3 spring onions (scallions)
butter
olive oil
2 potatoes sliced thinly

In a bowl, beat 8 eggs then add cheese and zucchini, seasoning and spring onions and set aside.

In a pan heat oil and butter then add the potatoes and cook them until they are soft, turning while cooking.

Once potatoes are cooked pour in egg mixture and reduce the heat. Cover the pan with a lid and cook for about 15 minutes. Turn onto a plate and slice ready to serve.

Tip

Asparagus is a great addition to this dish.

Carpaccio Di Manzo

MARINATED BEEF

PREPARATION TIME: 35 MINUTES

SERVES: 4

600g (1¹/₃ lbs) beef fillet, thinly sliced
sea salt and ground black pepper
30g (1oz) baby capers
3 tablespoon mayonnaise
2 handfuls rocket/aragula
1 tablespoon lemon juice

1 tablespoon extra virgin olive oil
salt and pepper
80g (3 oz) parmesan cheese, shaved
pane di casa or other crusty white bread,
* to serve*

Place beef between two pieces of cling film and flatten with a meat mallet. Set aside and repeat for all fillets.

To make caper mayonnaise, mix capers and mayonnaise together in a bowl. Cover with cling film and place in refrigerator.

Dress rocket with lemon juice, salt, pepper, and oil and place on top of beef. Grind over fresh black pepper and top with freshly shaved parmesan cheese. Serve with pane di casa, or other crusty white bread.

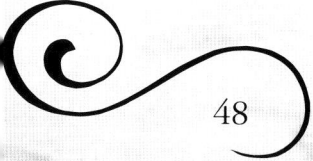

Quaglia Arrosta

GRILLED QUAIL

PREPARATION TIME: *20 MINUTES PLUS MARINATING*

COOKING TIME: *20 MINUTES*

SERVES: *4*

1 lemon, juiced	½ cup white wine vinegar
4 tablespoons olive oil	30ml (1 fl oz) white wine
1 garlic clove, crushed	salt and pepper
2 parsley sprigs, coarsley chopped	4 quails
2 rosemary sprigs,	lemon wedges to serve

In a bowl mix lemon juice, oil, garlic, parsley, rosemary, vinegar and wine and season with salt and pepper.

Rinse quails well under cool running water, dry and cut through the breast to butterfly, using the palm of your hand to flatten each quail. Place quails in the marinade and leave for at least 1 hour, or longer for stronger taste.

Line grill with foil to retain cooking juices. Cook quail under a hot griller for 7 minutes on each side, until golden, making sure they are about 15cm (6ins) from the heat. Serve with lemon wedges.

Buratta Salad
MOZZARELLA AND TOMATO SALAD

PREPARATION TIME: 25 MINUTES

SERVES: 4

150g (5¼oz) grape/cherry tomatoes,
   halved
50ml (1½ fl oz) extra virgin olive oil
pinch dried oregano
10 basil leaves, finely sliced
120g (4oz) ligurian or black olives
4 x 120g (4oz) balls buratta or
   mozzarella cheese
salt and freshly cracked pepper

BALSAMIC GLAZE
150ml (4½ fl oz) balsamic vinegar
1 cinnamon quill
1 star anise
65g (2oz) brown sugar

In a mixing bowl add tomatoes, oil, oregano, basil, olives, salt and pepper, toss gently. Place a buratta cheese ball in the centre of a plate and scatter tomatoes around.

To make balsamic glaze, add balsamic vinegar, cinnamon and star anise in a pot. Bring to the boil and then simmer until reduced by half. Remove cinnamon and star anise. Add sugar and reduce glaze by a quarter.

Drizzle tomatoes with balsamic glaze and season with cracked black pepper.

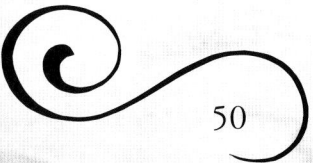

In many parts of Italy vongole are considered peasant food as they are so readily available.
Papá loved this diss.
No one could move from our dinner table after this dish it was so very satisfying.

Spaghetti Vongole

SPAGHETTI WITH CLAMS

PREPARATION TIME: *20 MINUTES*

COOKING TIME: *20 MINUTES*

SERVES: *6*

1kg (2lbs) clams
1 bunch parsley
3 garlic cloves
1 punnet cherry tomatoes

½ cup of white wine
salt and pepper
$\frac{1}{3}$ cup extra virgin olive oil
3 birdseye chillies, chopped

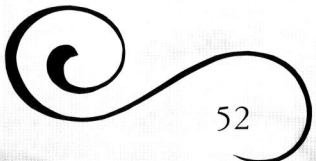

Cook spaghetti according to packet directions in a pot of boiling water.
Meanwhile, clean the clams.

In a large deep pan (with a lid), heat a generous serve of oil and add
garlic, chillies and chopped tomatoes. Toss to combine for a few minutes,
then add the clams and wine. Combine ingredients, then cover pan with
a lid. Within about 5 minutes the clams will open. Once pasta is cooked,
drain, reserving a cup of the water to add later if required. Add pasta to the
clams pan and toss in parsley. Serve, adding a drizzle of extra oil over the
dish if preferred.

Tip

Add extra chilli if you like it a little spicier! If you can time this dish well it
will be sensational, so really get a move on once the pasta is in the water
because you don't want to over cook your pasta, it must be al dente.

 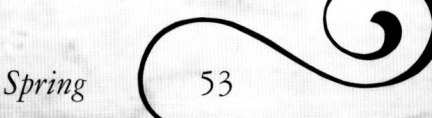

Papardelle e Capra Ragú

Pasta and goat sauce

Preparation time: 40 minutes

Cooking time: 2½ hours

Serves: 4

120g (4oz) plain flour (all-purpose flour)

800g (28oz) goat shoulder, cut into 3cm
  (1ins) pieces

120ml (4 fl oz) extra virgin olive oil

2 medium brown onion, diced

1 medium sized carrot, diced

2 celery stalks, diced

2 tablespoons tomato paste

1 cup red wine

1L (2 pints) chicken stock

½ cup peeled broad beans

2 sprigs marjoram, fresh, leaf only

800g (28oz) fresh papardelle pasta

60g (2oz) unsalted butter

60g (2oz) grated parmesan cheese

salt and pepper

5L (10 pints) water

100g (3½oz) salt

Lightly flour goat pieces. In a large pot, heat half the amount of oil until it starts to smoke then add goat. Reduce heat to medium and cook until goat is browned on all sides. Once coloured remove goat and set aside.

Add remaining oil to the pot with onion, celery and carrot. Sauté on medium low heat for 8-10 minutes without colouring the vegetables. Add tomato paste and cook for 3-4 minutes then add red wine, and simmer until sauce is reduced by three-quarters.

Add chicken stock and goat pieces, bring back to the boil and reduce to a simmer for approximately 2½ hours or until goat is tender and sauce has reduced by three-quarters and is almost thick in consistency. Season to taste.

Meanwhile, bring salted water to the boil and cook fresh pasta for 3 to 4 minutes with peeled broad beans. Drain, then add cooked pasta and beans to goat ragú with unsalted butter, marjoram and grated parmesan cheese and stirred through gently.

*In his older years, this was
Nonno's choice for a midday meal. Yet another
dish he attributed to his slender build.*

Pasta Ceci

PASTA WITH CHICKPEAS (GARBANZO BEANS)

PREPARATION TIME: *1 HOUR PLUS SOAKING*

COOKING TIME: *30 MINUTES*

SERVES: *4*

*250g (9oz) dried chickpeas (garbanzo
  beans)*
3 large celery stalks, chopped
1 garlic clove, crushed
1 birdseye chilli, diced
3 plump tomatoes, halved

salt and white pepper
a few parsley sprigs
60ml (2 fl oz) olive oil
1 packet of pasta, shell shaped is best

Soak the chickpeas overnight in enough water to cover.

Add chickpeas to a fresh pot of water and bring to a boil. After 15 minutes or once they are almost soft, drain and discard this water. Fill the pot with fresh water to cover chickpeas and cook again until tender, or to your liking, for about 10 minutes. Drain. Add celery, garlic, chilli, tomatoes and seasoning and cook covered on a medium heat for 20 minutes. Cook the pasta according to the directions on the packet to al dente. After 20 minutes add freshly chopped parsley and olive oil and serve on top of the pasta.

Tip
A short, shell shaped pasta goes well with this dish.

Braciole di Vitello

STUFFED VEAL ROLLS

PREPARATION TIME: *20 MINUTES*

COOKING TIME: *1½ HOURS*

SERVES: *10*

FILLING
500g (1lb) loaf unsliced white bread
200g (7oz) ham, finely diced
250g (9oz) (1¾ oz) (9oz) provolone,
  grated
1 bunch parsley, finely chopped
2 cloves garlic, finely chopped
40g (1½oz) unsalted butter, room
  temperature
salt and pepper

BRACIOLE
800g (28oz) veal schnitzel
100ml (3½ fl oz) extra virgin olive oil
2 metres (6½ ft) butchers string

Preheat oven to 180°C/350°F. Remove bread from crust and chop finely.
Add bread to a bowl and mix with the other finely chopped filling. Using
a meat mallet, flatten veal schnitzel and spoon mixture evenly down the
centre of the schnitzel.

   Fill and roll into a cigar shape, ensuring schnitzel rolls one and a half
times around. Tie with butcher's string, roll in plain flour and lightly fry.
Remove from frying pan and place rolls in an ovenproof dish. Finish in
oven for 8 minutes.

This is one of our childhood dishes.
Ma also added potato pieces, which would be
crunchy but soft at the same time.

Pollo alla Cacciatora

CHICKEN IN TOMATO SAUCE

PREPARATION TIME: *30 MINUTES*

COOKING TIME: *45 MINUTES*

SERVES: *4*

60ml (2 fl oz) extra virgin olive oil

30g (1oz) unsalted butter

1 whole chicken cut into pieces

1 medium brown onion, cut into rough dice

2 celery stalks, cut into rough dice

1 small carrot, cut into rough dice

6 medium tomatoes, peeled, deseeded and chopped

500ml (1 pint) chicken stock

½ cup white wine

salt and pepper

½ bunch parsley, finely chopped

In a large heavy based pot heat oil and butter, add chicken and onion and cook until golden. Once a nice golden colour has been achieved add celery, carrot, tomato and chicken stock, bring to the boil then reduce to a simmer for approximately 45 minutes until chicken is tender. Season to taste and finish with chopped parsley.

You can vary the amount of white wine and chicken stock, in some regions neither are used, and add mushrooms if liked. You can also cut 4 potatoes into wedges and place in the pot as chicken cooks.

Marinara Bianco

SEAFOOD IN WHITE WINE

PREPARATION TIME: *45 MINUTES*

COOKING TIME: *20 MINUTES*

SERVES: *4*

100ml (2½ fl oz) extra virgin olive oil

4 garlic cloves, sliced

1 chilli, sliced

180g (3 oz) octopus

180g (3 oz) calamari

8 shrimp/prawns, peeled, head removed

24 mussels

12 vongole

8 scallops

120ml (4 fl oz) white wine

4L (8 pints) water

50g (1¾ oz) salt

1 fennel bulb, including leaves

500g (1lb) spaghetti

In a cold pan add most of the olive oil keep a tablespoon aside. Add garlic and chilli. Heat on medium until garlic colours slightly. Add all of the seafood and cook covered with a lid until the mussels and vongole open. Remove shellfish from pan, take out the meat and discard shell. Return shellfish meat to sauce and add white wine.

In a large pot, bring water and salt to the boil, add fennel and cook until tender. Strain and keep the liquid to cook the spaghetti to packet directions until al dente. Strain pasta. Add cooked fennel and cooked pasta to seafood sauce. Toss through parsley, a tablespoon of olive oil and season to taste.

Cotolette alla Milanese

BREADED VEAL CUTLET

PREPARATION TIME: *40 MINUTES*

COOKING TIME: *22 MINUTES*

SERVES: *4*

4 x 250g (9oz) rib eye veal cutlet

200g (7oz) plain flour (all-purpose flour)

3 eggs

120ml (4fl oz) milk

250g (9oz) breadcrumbs

60g (2oz) parmesan cheese, grated

½ bunch parsley, finely chopped

pinch dried oregano

salt and pepper

80g (3 oz) butter, unsalted

40ml (1¹/₃ fl oz) extra virgin olive oil

Preaheat oven to 180°C/350°F. Season rib eye and and dust with flour. In a bowl, combine egg and milk, and dip cutlets into egg mixture. In another bowl, combine breadcrumbs, parmesan cheese, parsley and oregano. Place cutlets in crumb mixture, patting firmly to make sure crumb sticks. In a frying pan, heat butter and olive oil over medium to high heat, until it starts to bubble. Add cutlets and cook until golden on both sides.

Remove cutlets from frying pan and place on an oven tray and cook in oven for approximately 4 minutes. Best served with a lemon wedge, mixed leaf salad, cherry tomato, onion, balsamic vinegar and extra virgin olive oil.

Cannoli

ITALIAN CUSTARD PASTRY

Cannoli Shell

PREPARATION TIME: 1 HOUR 5 MINUTES

COOKING TIME: 1 HOUR 45 MINUTES

MAKES: 10 PIECES

1¹/₃ cups plain flour (all-purpose flour)	*pinch salt*
pinch cinnamon	*½ cup marsala*
1 tablespoon shortening (lard)	*egg white*
½ teaspoon caster sugar (superfine sugar)	*vegetable oil for deep frying*

Combine the flour, cinnamon, shortening, sugar and salt. Wetting gradually with the wine, knead together with fingers until a fairly hard paste or dough is formed. Roll into a ball, cover with a cloth and set aside to stand for about 1 hour. Cut dough in half and roll half of the dough into a thin sheet about ¼ inch thick (6mm) or less and cut into 4 inch (12cm) ovals. Place a metal tube diagonally across each oval lengthwise. Wrap dough around tube by overlapping the 2 sides, sealing the overlapping sides with a little egg white. Meanwhile, heat vegetable oil in a large deep pan for deep frying. Drop 1 or 2 of the tubes at a time into the hot oil, fry gently on all sides until dough turns a golden brown.

Remove from pan, allow to cool slightly before gently removing shell from the metal tube. Set shells aside to cool fully. Repeat with remaining dough mixture.

Ricotta Filling for Cannoli

PREPARATION TIME: *15 MINUTES*

COOKING TIME: *35 MINUTES*

MAKES: *10 PORTIONS, APPROXIMATELY 1 LITRE (32 FL OZ)*

*65g (2oz) dark chocolate
   (semisweet chocolate)*
1 teaspoon vanilla essence

120g (4 oz) icing sugar
850g (2lb) ricotta

Add finely grated chocolate, vanilla essence and icing sugar to ricotta. Whisk until all are combined and smooth in texture. Refrigerate for 2 hours before using. To fill cannoli, place ricotta into a pipping bag and pipe evenly into each end of the cannoli shells.

Vanilla Custard Filling for Cannoli

PREPARATION TIME: *25 MINUTES*

SETTING TIME: *4 HOURS*

MAKES: *10 PORTIONS, APPROXIMATELY 1 LITRE (32 FL OZ)*

330ml (11fl oz) milk

70g (2½ oz) caster sugar (superfine sugar)

65g (2oz) cornflour (cornstarch)

1 egg, lightly beaten

2 teaspoons super montigo (or rum)

165ml (5½fl oz) thickened cream

1 teaspoon lacrime (or other Italian liqueur, such as Sambucca)

1 teaspoon vanilla essence

In a large pan, heat 250ml (8fl oz) of milk and 35g (1¼oz) sugar. Place remaining milk into a separate bowl and mix in remaining sugar, cornflour and lightly beaten egg. Strain through a fine sieve.

Once milk comes to boil, add milk and egg mix and whisk vigorously for 1 minute to cook egg through. Tip into a mixing bowl and whip until cold, then cover with cling film and allow to set in the refrigerator for about 4 hours.

Once cool, whisk thickened cream until firm then gradually add to cooled custard. Mix with liqueurs and vanilla essence.

To fill cannoli, place custard into a pipping bag and pipe evenly into each end of the cannoli shells.

Chocolate Custard Filling for Cannoli

PREPARATION TIME: 25 MINUTES

SETTING TIME: 4 HOURS

MAKES: 10 PORTIONS, APPROXIMATELY 1 LITRE (32 FL OZ)

330ml (11fl oz) milk

70g (2½ oz) caster sugar (superfine sugar)

65g (2oz) cornflour (cornstarch)

1 egg, lightly beaten

1 teaspoon vanilla essence

165ml (5½fl oz) thickened cream

20g (¾oz) dark Dutch cocoa

In a large pan, heat 250ml (8fl oz) of milk and 35g (1¼oz) sugar. Place remaining milk into a separate bowl and mix in remaining sugar, cornflour and lightly beaten egg. Strain through a fine sieve.

Once milk comes to boil, add milk and egg mix and whisk vigorously for 1 minute to cook egg through. Tip into a mixing bowl and whip until cold, then cover with cling film and allow to set in the refrigerator for about 4 hours.

Once cool, whisk thickened cream until firm then gradually add to cooled custard. Mix in cocoa and vanilla essence while whisking until fully incorporated. To fill cannoli, place custard into a pipping bag and pipe evenly into each end of the cannoli shells.

Tiramisu

ITALIAN CREAM CAKE

PREPARATION TIME: **20** MINUTES

COOKING TIME: **20** MINUTES, PLUS COOLING

SERVES: 8

4 eggs, separated
⅔ cup of caster sugar (superfine sugar)
500g (1lb) mascarpone cheese or other
  soft cheese
1 tablespoon Italian liqueur, such as
  Strega or Sambucca

¼ cup Vermouth
6 cups espresso coffee, slightly cooled
400g (14oz) Italian sponge finger
  biscuits

Beat egg yolks and ⅓ cup sugar in a bowl until thick and creamy. In a separate bowl mix egg whites with ⅓ cup of sugar until stiff. Fold the egg white into the yolks and then fold in the mascarpone cheese. Add the liqueur and fold in the mixture.

Mix the vermouth with the coffee. Dip the biscuits one at a time in coffee mixture and place a layer of them into a rectangular dish. Cover with layer of the mascarpone cheese mixture.

Repeat with another layer of biscuits and mascarpone mixture. Sprinkle with powdered cocoa. Store in fridge until firm. This dish is best made a day ahead.

Limone Biscotti

LEMON BISCUITS WITH ICING

PREPARATION TIME: 50 MINUTES

COOKING TIME: 25 MINUTES

MAKES: 60 BISCOTTI

8 eggs

2 cups white sugar

250g (9oz) unsalted butter (melted and
    cooled)

250ml (8½ oz) carton cream
    (or 1 cup of milk)

1 tablespoon vanilla essence

1 tablespoon lemon essence or Limoncello

rind of 2 lemons, grated

1.5kg (3lbs) self-raising flour, sifted, plus
    extra if required

LEMON ICING

1kg (2lbs) icing sugar, sifted

½ to ¾ cup of boiling water

lemon essence or Limoncello

Heat oven to 180°C/350°F. Line at least 4 trays with baking paper.

Beat the eggs, adding sugar and melted butter, then add cream (or milk), vanilla essence, lemon essence and lemon rind.

Slowly fold in sifted flour till the dough is manageable, add a little more flour if you think it's too sticky because you will be kneading by hand. Dough should be soft but easy to handle so that you can shape it. Make into desired shapes (fingers, circles or cookies) and place on prepared trays.

Bake in oven until very lightly browned (these biscuits should be soft inside) for approximately 15 minutes. Put the biscuits to one side to cool.

Meanwhile, make the icing. Pour ½ cup boiling water into a bowl, add the icing sugar a little at a time, then mix until smooth until the icing sugar has the consistency of pouring cream, adding extra water if needed. Add the lemon essence last, as pouring boiling water over the essence will dilute the lemon flavour.

Coat either the top or the entire biscuit in icing and allow to set before storing in an airtight container.

 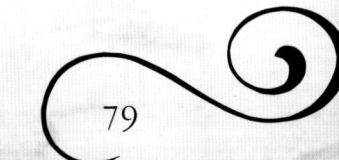

Cuzzupe

CALABRESE EASTER CAKE

Cuzzupe is a Calabrese celebration cake a little like Brioche, and is often baked at Easter. This recipe was Nonna's and is over 80 years old. The yeast she used was left-over dough from the previous day's bread baking.

At Easter time Nonna would make special biscuits and cakes as they could not afford chocolate, which was a rarity in their village. She would bake a Cuzzupe for each child and place it in a basket in the shape of a wreath adorned with three eggs, which were each marked with a cross to hold them in place.

Each child argued over whose basket was biggest!

Preparation time: 2 hours

Cooking time:

Serves: 8

7 fresh eggs plus one egg yolk

200g (7oz) sugar

1 cup milk

1½ sachets dried yeast
   (2¼ teaspoons each)

1kg (2lbs) plain flour (all-purpose flour)

1 cup olive oil

lemon rind

vanilla essence

Preheat the oven to 180°C/350°F.

Beat 4 eggs and sugar in a bowl.

Warm milk on the stove or in microwave. Add milk, eggs and sugar to a bowl with the dry yeast and flour and mix together to form a dough. Once combined allow to sit and rise for an hour. Then commence to roll it into 2 long logs an inch (3cm) wide. Then twist the two long strips together and form them into a circle shape.

Allow this circle of dough to sit for a further hour so that it may rise again.

Add 3 whole fresh eggs to the top of the dough and with left over dough form a cross on top of the eggs to act as a handle holding the eggs in place (this is more an aesthetic touch and not really to hold the eggs in place, the dough will do that). Brush the whole circle of dough with an egg yolk and sprinkle sugar over for a brown, lightly glazed effect. Bake in the preheated oven for 45 minutes.

Summer

Starter

Figs wrapped in ham and cheese

Octopus salad

Fish cakes

Side

Orange and shellfish salad

Vegetables in olive oil

Fig salad

Aeolian salad

Polenta with Napolitana sauce

Pasta

Chilli and shellfish spaghetti

*Linguine with anchovies, capers,
   olives and breadcrumbs*

Main Course

Mussels in white wine

Sweet

Custard pastry

Small profiteroles

Panna cotta

Holidays

Our summer holidays were always short-lived as Papá had to return to work. Instead of continuing our trips to the beach and staying up late, we found ourselves in the back of Papá's truck, giving him a hand at work laying pebblecrete. The rest of the school holidays consisted of manual labour and helping Papá source the tomatoes for the annual ritual: making the salsa pomodoro (tomato sauce). We did this in summer when the tomatoes were ripe and good value and we'd keep them for the whole winter, when the tomatoes were scarce (see Basic recipes). It was a family event where all the aunties and cousins would gather at our house as early as 3am because the process needed to be completed in a day (you couldn't leave tomatoes resting in barrels as they would become too acidic). This was an enjoyable family event, with everyone sharing stories, reminiscing and joking.

Anyone would think that making sugo was an easy task or at least a matter of heading down to the vegetable markets and buying a truckload of tomatoes, but not for Papá. It was almost like choosing a champion thoroughbred racehorse.

Step number one: the tomatoes had to be purchased from a trusted source that would ensure the quality of tomatoes and consistency required to make the perfect Criniti sauce.

There was a lot at stake, since much of the sauce would be given away to family and friends, and of course be judged. God forbid someone else's sauce was given more votes than my Papá's.

Being a Criniti means striving for perfection, a philosophy which applied to everything we did. Papá always said if you do something, do it to the best of your ability, with the same energy and determination. Then you can never be disappointed in yourself.

1968: Papa Cosimo Criniti enjoying a T-bone steak on his honeymoon.

Once the tomatoes were brought home, step two
began: cleaning and preparing the garage, where
the sauce would be made. We sterilised that
garage like it was an operating theatre.
On the morning of the annual sauce making day
everyone had strict instructions, and Frank was in
charge of washing the bottles.
This was a meticulous process undertaken with
bottle cleaner in hand, glass bottle in the other,
watched over by the adults to ensure my work was
up to scratch.

Our sisters and cousins were in charge of washing the tomatoes and our youngest brother had the difficult task of adding the single leaf of basil to each bottle before it was sealed.

The preparation and preservation of food didn't stop with tomatoes. Ma would also preserve eggplants (aubergines) and zucchinis (courgettes), placing them in jars and then adding oregano, oil and garlic. Apart from being economical, food preservation also gave everything our mother's loving touch, which made us enjoy them even more.

Fichi, Proscuitto e Gorgonzola

FIGS WRAPPED IN HAM AND CHEESE

PREPARATION TIME: 25 MINUTES

COOKING TIME: 12 MINUTES

SERVES: 4

12 figs

12 slices proscuitto

300ml (10 fl oz) cream

100g (3½ oz) gorgonzola piccante or
  other soft white cheese

50g (1¾oz) grated parmesan cheese

½ bunch parsley, finely chopped

Preheat the oven to 180°C/350°F. Cut off the tops and bottoms of the figs, and wrap with proscuitto. Place in oven for 3 minutes.

Meanwhile, in a pan bring the cream and gorgonzola to the boil and reduce by a half. Add parmesan cheese and chopped parsley and cook until the mixture has thickened slightly.

Remove the figs from the oven and place on a plate. Pour over gorgonzola sauce to serve.

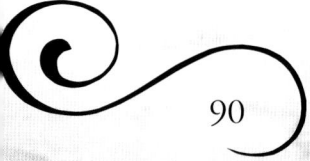

Insalata di Polipi
OCTOPUS SALAD

PREPARATION TIME: *25 MINUTES*

COOKING TIME: *35 MINUTES*

SERVES: *4*

5L (10 pints) water

100g (3½ oz) salt

50ml (1½ fl oz) lemon juice

100ml (3½ fl oz) white wine vinegar

100ml (3½ fl oz) white wine

20 black peppercorns

1kg (2lbs) octopus tentacles

*6 medium desiree potatoes, peeled and
  diced*

500g (1lb) baby spinach leaves

20g (¾ oz) baby capers

100ml (3½ fl oz) extra virgin olive oil

1 birdseye chilli, sliced thinly

30ml (1 fl oz) lemon juice

salt and pepper

Place water, salt, lemon juice, white wine vinegar, white wine, black peppercorns and octopus into a large pot. Bring to boil and reduce to a simmer for approximately 35 minutes or until octopus is tender.

Remove from water and set aside to cool.

Meanwhile, boil the diced potatoes in salted water until tender. Slice the octopus in rings or as desired.

Place in a bowl with cooked potato, spinach and capers. Dress with extra virgin olive oil, chilli, lemon juice, salt and pepper.

Nanata Fritters

FISH CAKES

PREPARATION TIME: 35 MINUTES PLUS RESTING TIME 1 HOUR

COOKING TIME: 20 MINUTES

MAKES: 10

1kg (2 lbs) silver fish (whitebait)
400g (14 oz) plain flour
  (all-purpose flour)
2 eggs
200ml (7 fl oz) milk
50ml (1½ fl oz) water
100g (3½ oz) grated parmesan cheese

3½ tablespoons chilli oil
3½ tablespoons garlic oil
1 bunch parsley, finely chopped
15 basil leaves, finely chopped
salt and pepper, to taste
2L (4 pints) cottonseed oil

Place all ingredients, except cottonseed oil, in a mixing bowl and mix by hand until all are combined well. Cover with cling film and allow to rest for 1 hour in the refrigerator.

Heat a pot with cottonseed oil to 180°C/350°F. Shape the fish mixture into dumplings with two teaspoons and drop gently into the hot oil. Fry for approximately 4 minutes, turning constantly until golden brown. Remove from oil and drain on paper towel. Season with salt.

Serve with a fresh green salad.

Insalata Arancia con Gamberi

ORANGE AND SHELLFISH SALAD

PREPARATION TIME: 35 MINUTES

COOKING TIME: 15 MINUTES

SERVES: 4

24 medium sized cooked shrimp/prawns

8 navel oranges, peeled and segmented

50g (1¾ oz) baby capers in brine

100g (3½ oz) rocket/aragula

2 celery stalks, roughly chopped

40ml (1¹/₃ fl oz) white wine vinegar

80ml (2²/₃ fl oz) extra virgin olive oil

salt and ground black pepper

1 Spanish (purple) onion, sliced into rings

12 celery leaves, to garnish

Peel cooked prawns and place in a bowl. Add remaining ingredients, season, and toss well. Divide over four plates, add onion rings and celery leaves to garnish.

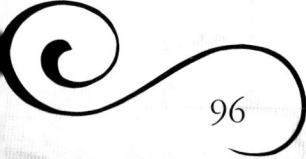

Caponata

VEGETABLES IN OLIVE OIL

PREPARATION TIME: 30 MINUTES

COOKING TIME: 55 MINUTES

SERVES: 4

150ml (4 fl oz) extra virgin olive oil

2 medium sized eggplant/aubergine

1 medium brown onion

2 celery stalks

1 medium sized red capsicum/bell pepper

60g (2oz) flaked almonds, roasted

60ml (2 fl oz) white wine vinegar

2 medium tomatoes, peeled

120g (4 oz) sultanas

¼ bunch parsley, finely chopped

4 basil leaves to garnish

salt and pepper

Cut aubergine, onion, celery, bell pepper and tomatoes into 3cm x 3cm (1in x 1in) cubes.

In a pan, heat 100ml (3½ fl oz) olive oil and fry aubergine until golden on both sides. Remove from pan and place on paper towel. Heat remaining oil in pan and fry onion, celery and capsicum until soft. Add vinegar, sultanas and tomato and cook until vinegar has reduced by about half, for 7 to 9 minutes. Then add fried eggplant, roasted flaked almonds and chopped parsley. Season to taste with salt and pepper. Granish with basil. Serve either hot or cold, although it is traditionally enjoyed cold. Great on it's own or accompanying meats and seafood.

 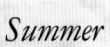

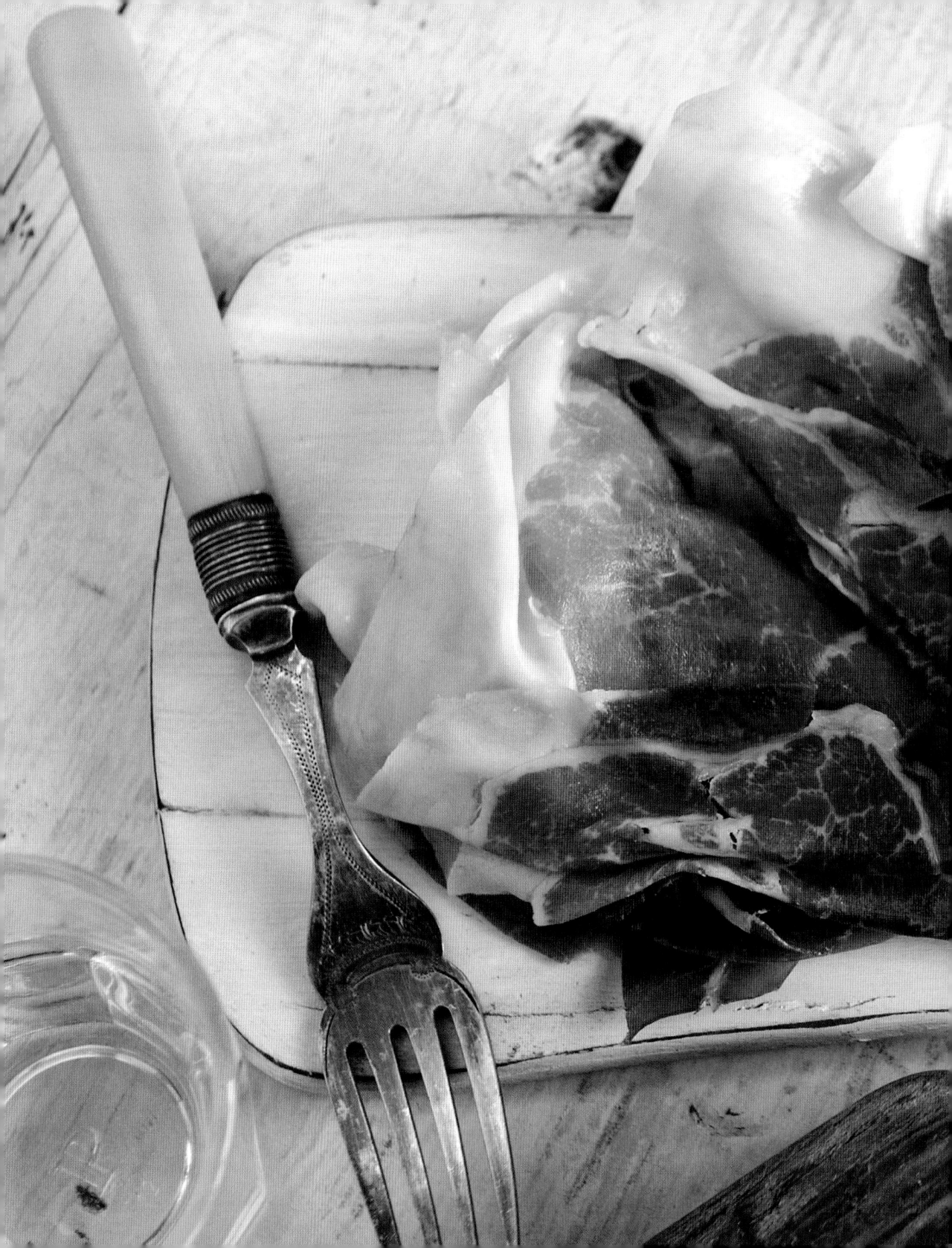

Insalata di Fichi

FIG SALAD

PREPARATION TIME: 25 MINUTES

SERVES: 4

60g (2 oz) pinenuts

100g (3½ oz) walnuts, roasted

8 figs, quartered

150g (5¼ oz) green grapes

400g (14 oz) fresh ricotta

400g (14 oz) wild rocket

80ml (2 ⅔ fl oz) extra virgin olive oil

salt and pepper

In a pan, dry roast pinenuts and walnuts until golden. Allow to cool. Quarter figs and combine with all remaining ingredients in a large mixing bowl. Season to taste and serve immediately.

This is a typical dish from the Aeolian Islands in Sicily, where the locals prefer to use fresh local ingredients like fish, capers and local herbs to create simple but delicious food.

Aeolian Salad

PREPARATION TIME: *15 minutes*

SERVES SIZE: *2*

4 medium truss tomatoes

1 white onion, sliced into rings

1 medium eggplant/aubergine, cut into
  cubes

200ml (7 fl oz) cottonseed oil

20g (¾ oz) baby capers

200g (7 oz) tuna, canned, in brine

pinch dried oregano

50ml (1½ fl oz) extra virgin olive oil

1½ tablespoons white wine vinegar

salt and pepper

70g (2½ oz) focaccia

Quarter the truss tomatoes and place in a bowl with white onion rings, baby capers, white wine vinegar, tuna, oregano, olive oil and season to taste.

Allow to rest for 15 minutes. Meanwhile in a pan, fry eggplant cubes in cottonseed oil until golden brown. Remove from pan and place on paper towel to absorb any extra oil.

Cut foccacia into 2cm (¾ in) cubes and toast in the oven until golden brown. Add the fried eggplant and toasted crouton to the salad mixture and toss.

Divide over two plates and serve immediately.

Polenta con Sugo di Pomodoro

POLENTA WITH NAPOLITANA SAUCE

PREPARATION TIME: 40 MINUTES

COOKING TIME: 35 MINUTES

SERVES: 4

2L (4 pints) water

pinch of salt

60ml (2 fl oz) olive oil

80g (3 oz) butter

400g (14 oz) polenta

60g (2 oz) parmesan cheese

300ml (10 fl oz) Napolitana sauce
  (see Basic Recipes)

8 basil leaves

In a pot bring the water, salt, olive oil and butter to a rapid boil. Whisk in the polenta and reduce heat to low. Continue to stir until the polenta is smooth. Mix in parmesan cheese, remove from heat and set aside.

Heat napolitana sauce and place in a bowl. Pour polenta mix over the top, garnish with basil leaves and serve immediately.

Spaghetti con gamberi e peperoncino

CHILLI AND SHELLFISH SPAGHETTI

PREPARATION TIME: *10 MINUTES*

COOKING TIME: *12 MINUTES*

SERVES: *4*

80ml (2 fl oz) extra virgin olive oil
1 garlic, thinly sliced
2 hot chillis, thinly sliced
500g (1lbs) shrimp/prawns

500g (1lb) packet spaghetti
½ bunch parsley, finely chopped to serve
salt and pepper

Bring a saucepan of water to the boil and drop the pasta in. Add half a teaspoon of salt and cook until it is al dente.

Meanwhile, in a frying pan, add olive oil and garlic and chilli. Heat until the garlic lightly colours. Add the shrimp and cook for 3-4 minutes until they are slightly pink.

Turn off the heat and season shrimp with salt and pepper. Drain the spaghetti and return it to the saucepan. Add the shrimp and stir through. Garnish with parsley.

Tip

You can also add half a can of cherry tomatoes to this dish. When the shrimp are cooked, remove from pan leaving the garlic and chilli and cook for 8 minutes.

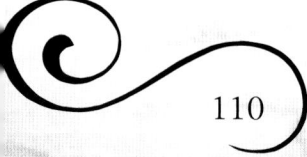

In Calabria, this dish is also traditionally eaten on Christmas Eve.

Linguine al Mollica

LINGUINE WITH ANCHOVIES, CAPERS, OLIVES AND BREADCRUMBS

PREPARATION TIME: 15 MINUTES

COOKING TIME: 20 MINUTES

SERVES: 6

1 packet linguine pasta

olive oil

¼ cup anchovies

¼ cup capers

¼ cup black olives

2 birdseye chillies, finely sliced

2 garlic cloves, finely sliced

½ cup breadcrumbs

Heat oven to 160°C/320°F. Bring a pot of water to the boil and cook linguine according to packet directions until al dente. Meanwhile, mix breadcrumbs and oil in a heatproof casserole dish and bake for 10 minutes.

Heat oil in a pan, add olives, chillies, garlic, capers and anchovies, and cook stirring over medium heat until the anchovies are dissolved.

Drain the pasta and toss in the anchovy sauce.

Transfer the dish with the breadcrumbs to the stove top. Add the pasta and sauce to the top of the breadcrumbs and fry for 1 minute over medium heat. Then invert the dish onto a large plate. Cut into portions and serve.

Cozze Bianco

MUSSELS IN WHITE WINE

PREPARATION TIME: 20 MINUTES

COOKING TIME: 14 MINUTES

SERVES: 4

60ml (2 fl oz) extra virgin olive oil
2 garlic cloves, thinly sliced
1 birdseye chilli, thinly sliced
½ medium brown onion, diced
60ml (2 fl oz) white wine

2kg (4lbs) mussels
400ml (16½ fl oz) fish stock
1 bunch parsley, finely chopped
salt and pepper

In a large pan or wok heat oil, garlic, chilli and onion and saute for 5 to 6 minutes. Add white wine, mussels and fish stock. Cover with a lid and cook for 10 minutes.

Remove mussels from pan, discarding any that have not opened and continue to simmer the liquid.

Remove mussel meat from shells. Place mussel meat in a separate bowl.

Reduce liquid by half by simmering. Add chopped parsley and mussel meat as well as some of the shells to liquid, and season with salt and pepper to taste.

Cartocci

CUSTARD PASTRY

PREPARATION TIME: *3 HOURS INCLUDING RESTING*

COOKING TIME: *45 MINUTES*

MAKES: *20 PIECES*

400ml (16½ fl oz) milk

4 eggs

125g (4½ oz) unsalted butter at room
    temperature

90g (3 oz) caster sugar (superfine sugar)

1 teaspoon table salt

1kg (2lbs) plain flour
    (all-purpose flour)

zest of 1 lemon

30g (1oz) fresh yeast

2L (4 pints) cottonseed oil

100g (3½ oz) icing mixture

50g (1¾ oz) extra caster sugar
    (superfine sugar)

2 teaspoons ground cinnamon

2½ teaspoons ground nutmeg

1kg (2lbs) cannoli filling custard
    (see Cannoli recipe)

Place milk, eggs and butter into a mixing bowl. Add sugar, salt, flour, lemon
zest and yeast and mix until it has the consistancy of a glutenous dough.
Cover and place in the fridge for about 2 hours to prove. Roll out as thinly
as possible, and cut into 5cm (2ins) strips. Roll each piece of dough around
a cannoli stick, remove, and allow to prove for another hour.

In a deep pan, heat oil to 180°C/350°F and fry pastry until golden brown.
Mix caster sugar, cinnamon and nutmeg and roll fried pastries in sugar
mixture. Fill with custard as per Cannoli recipe.

 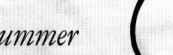

Bigne

SMALL PROFITEROLES

PREPARATION TIME: 45 MINUTES

COOKING TIME: 50 MINUTES

MAKES: 10

600ml (15 fl oz) water

200ml (7 fl oz) milk

60g (2 oz) caster sugar (superfine sugar)

300g (10 oz) unsalted butter

400g (14 oz) plain flour
   (all-purpose flour)

14 eggs

FILLING

1kg (2lbs) vanilla or chocolate cannoli
   filling custard (see Cannoli recipe)
   or Chantilly cream

CHANTILLY CREAM

200ml (5 oz) thickened cream

50g (1¾ oz) caster sugar (superfine sugar)

1 teaspoon vanilla essence

Preheat oven to 160°C/320°F. In a large pot add water, milk, sugar and butter and bring to the boil. Add flour and mix until it forms a dough and does not stick to sides of the pot. Remove dough mixture from pot and place in the bowl of an electric mixer. Add eggs one at a time, until each egg is incorporated into the mixture.

Pipe mixture into desired size on a tray covered with oiled baking paper. Bake for approximately 1 hour and 15 minutes. Allow to cool and fill with either chocolate or vanilla custard or Chantilly cream.

To make Chantilly cream, whip thickened cream with caster sugar and vanilla essence until stiff peaks form.

*This is a simple recipe to make
and a classic Italian dish.*

Panna Cotta

COOKED CREAM

PREPARATION TIME: 10 MINUTES

COOKING TIME: 10 MINUTES

SERVES: 8

600ml (15 fl oz) thickened cream
½ cup sugar
1 vanilla bean pod
3 teaspoons gelatin
¼ cup boiled water

TOPPING
¼ cup icing sugar
1 orange, juiced
½ punnet blueberries

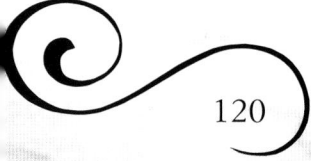

Pour cream, sugar and vanilla pod (cut open and scraped) into a deep pot on medium heat. Stir gently until the sugar has dissolved and the cream is heated through—do not boil.

In a bowl, add boiling water to gelatin and dissolve thoroughly. Add to the cream mixture and combine well ensuring that the gelatin has dissolved completely.

Remove from the stovetop. Remove the vanilla bean pod and pour mixture into 8 ramekin dishes. Refrigerate for 4 - 6 hours.

Meanwhile, prepare the toppings. Combine all the toppings ingredients together and refrigerate until required.

Once the Panna Cotta are set, simply turn onto a serving plate and spoon over the topping.

Tip

You can use any combination for a topping—traditionally in southern Italy Panna Cotta is topped with citrus.

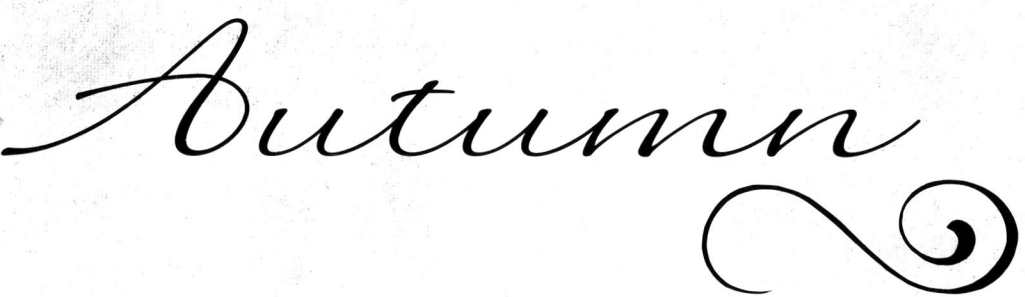

Autumn

Starter
Fried rice balls with cheese
Aubergine and cheese
Rice with peas, prosciutto
  and Italian cheese
Fried potato and anchovy
  dumplings

Side
Calabrese tomato salad
Cauliflower fritters
Fennel salad

Pasta
Pasta with peas
Pasta with Italian beans
Pasta bake
Pasta with cannellini beans

Main Course
Beef fillet with olive oil, lemon,
  herb and garlic sauce
Chicken breasts with marsala
Chicken in white wine
Veal schnitzel
Veal stew

Sweet
Ricotta cheesecake

Baking
Pistachio biscuits
Aunt Vittoria's lemon
  and almond biscuits

1977: Family picnic at Serra San Bruno

My Papá
Frank Criniti

Papá was the youngest of ten children, and my Nonno was a farmer and labourer who would work long hours ploughing the fields and planting wheat, so that his family would have enough wheat and bread for the whole year. They were not a wealthy family, but they were close. My father was closest to his two younger sisters, Carmela and Lucia.

When he was a boy, Papá would come home from school at midday and have lunch with his family, typically whatever was leftover, anchovies, olives and bread mostly. My Zias (aunts) would go to the local seamstress to learn how to sew, whilst my Zios (uncles) and Papá worked on the farm with my Nonno. The evening meal was most often pasta with seasonal vegetables; broadbeans, artichokes and cannellini beans. The family rarely ate meat, as it was a rare and special treat. Occasionally, Papá would visit his Zia and cousins. He would look forward to this as they would go to the river with his cousins, or the farm and pick fruit. Every year there would be a festival for Santa Caterina and other patron saints in Italy. To celebrate they would have a huge family lunch, and Nonna would treat them with pasta with meatballs or ragu.

Papà's fondest memories of Santa Caterina was helping his father to harvest the wheat. They'd put the wheat in bundles so that they could get it ready to make the family's bread. My Nonna and Zia would get up at 5am to bake the bread for the whole week. All their bread was made from the wheat that Nonno had grown and ground by hand. They did not have yeast, so every time they made bread they would set aside a piece of dough that would form the sourdough for their next bread making day.

At night, the family would sit with their neighbours and play games. Although they were not wealthy, they were always doing something together – a tradition that Papa carried on to his own family and one that we've continued.

Papá Cosimo Criniti's first car: a Ford Falcon.

Nonna Raffaela was a beautiful, fair-skinned woman who made it her life's mission to feed us until we could not longer fit in another morsel. Ma would send us over to her house and once in there, the doors were locked behind us until we ate everything she put in front of us. We'd eat soup, pizza, anchovies, and Brescoli di Riso (fried rice dumplings). We'd never exit empty-handed either; Nonna would send us away with a 'Dio vi Benedica' (May God bless you) and some money, socks, and anything else she could give us. Most times, we'd return home with a pot of her Sugo di Pomodoro, which usually sparked a debate over whose sugo was the tastiest, hers or Ma's. There was never any competition; Papa's was the best by far.

There were many occasions where Nonna and Ma cooked together and watching this, you were able to see and truly appreciate the ancestry and tradition that our food offered us. As they spoke in the Calabrese dialect (probably about Nonno's obsession with Baccala), they made fried lemon biscotti. It was Nonna who passed on her passion for cooking onto my mother and that's where we then inherited ours.

Nonno Domenico Pelli in his vegetable garden

Brescoli di Riso

FRIED RICE BALLS WITH CHEESE

PREPARATION TIME: 30 MINUTES PLUS COOLING

COOKING TIME: 25 MINUTES

MAKES: 10 PORTIONS

1kg (2lbs) Arborio rice

2¼L water (4½ pints)

60ml (2 fl oz) extra virgin olive oil

4 eggs

1½ cup grated parmesan cheese

½ cup parsley, finely chopped

400g (14 oz) breadcrumb

2L (4 pints) cottonseed oil

salt and pepper to taste

Napolitana Sauce (see Basic Recipes)

In a large pot, place rice in water and bring to a boil. Cook until the rice is soft and starchy, then drain and allow to cool. Once cooled add rice to a bowl with 4 eggs, parmesan cheese, parsley, salt and pepper and combine well. Rice mixture should now be very sticky in consistency. Hand mould approximately 3 tablespoons of mixture into cylinder shapes. Place on a large plate and allow to set in the fridge for about 2 hours.

Once set, roll rice balls in breadcrumbs. In a shallow frypan, heat cottonseed oil to 180°C/350°F and fry until brescoli are golden in colour. Remove and place on paper towel and season to taste. Serve with Napolitana sauce on side.

Tip

For extra crispy brescioli, double crumb before frying.

Melanzane Parmigiano

AUBERGINE AND CHEESE

PREPARATION TIME: 35 MINUTES

COOKING TIME: 35 MINUTES

SERVES: 4

3 eggplant/aubergine

120ml (4fl oz) olive oil

500ml (1 pint) Napolitana sauce

  (see Basic Recipes)

100ml (3½ fl oz) mozarella

100g (3½ oz) parmesan cheese

10 basil leaves

salt

Preheat oven to 180°C/350°F. Cut aubergine into 2½cm (¾ins) thick slices. Heat olive oil in a pan and fry aubergine until both sides are tender. Place onto absorbent paper to drain off excess oil.

On a small baking tray, cover the bottom with aubergine, then Napolitana sauce, mozzarella, parmesan cheese and salt. Continue layers until aubergine is finished and ensure that the top layer is mozzarella. Garnish with basil and bake for approximately 20 minutes. Once golden brown, remove from the oven and serve.

Risotto piselli con Prosciutto e Scamorza

RICE WITH PEAS, PROSCIUTTO AND ITALIAN CHEESE

PREPARATION TIME: 45 *MINUTES*

COOKING TIME: 50 *MINUTES*

SERVES: 10

900ml (30 fl oz) chicken stock

60ml (2 fl oz) extra virgin olive oil

1 small brown onion, finely diced

600g (1¹/₃ lbs) risotto rice

160g (5oz) prosciutto, cut in chunks

100g (3½oz) fresh or frozen peas for puree

100g (3½oz) peas, cooked

80g (3 oz) grated parmesan cheese

100g (3½ oz) scamorza or other soft
*   white cheese cut into cubes*

salt and pepper

In a pan, heat chicken stock. In a separate pot, sauté onion in olive oil for approximately 2 minutes then add rice and cook another 4-5 minutes while stirring continuously. Gradually add hot stock and lower to a medium heat, stirring only occasionally.

Defrost peas and blend in a food processor with 30ml (1 fl oz) of water until smooth in consistency. Once liquid has been absorbed add prosciutto, pea puree, cooked peas, parmesan cheese and scamorza. Stir through for 10-15 minutes. Season to taste with salt and pepper.

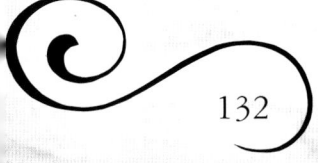

*This is a traditional dish also enjoyed by southern
Italians at Christmas time.*

Zeppole

FRIED POTATO AND ANCHOVY DUMPLINGS

PREPARATION TIME: *20* MINUTES

COOKING TIME: *30* MINUTES

MAKES: *20-25* DUMPLINGS

3 potatoes peeled and diced

*1½ kilos (3lbs) plain flour
    (all-purpose flour)*

1½ tablespoons salt

2 packets dried yeast

200ml (7fl oz) cottonseed oil

*½ cup of diced anchovies, or ½ cup of
    grilled capsicum/bell peppers cut into
    slices,*

Boil potatoes and when they are soft, mash them. Add the flour, salt and yeast. Combine well, then set aside with a tea towel over the bowl. Allow mix to prove for 1 hour. After the dough has risen, heat oil in a deep fryer. Add anchovies or peppers to the potato mixture. Scoop a handful and form into a doughnut or log shape.

Fry them in the deep fryer or in very hot oil and cook until golden.

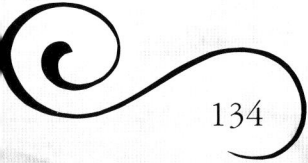

Insalata Calabrese

Calabrese tomato salad

Preparation time: 15 minutes

Serves: 4

16 Roma tomatoes, quartered

8 medium round tomatoes, cut into
  eighths

1 punnet (250g) cherry tomatoes

250g (9oz) ligurian (black) olives

2 large Spanish (purple) onions, sliced in
  to rings

3 birdseye chillies, sliced thinly

4 cloves garlic, sliced thinly

250ml (1½ fl oz) extra virgin olive oil,
  plus 80ml (2 ²/₃ fl oz) extra

20 basil leaves, torn

1 teaspoon dried oregano

salt and pepper

4 slices Pane Duro or other crusty Italian
  bread

100ml (3½ fl oz) water

Place all ingredients, except half a teaspoon of dried oregano, bread and salt, into a stainless steel bowl. Semi squash some of the tomatoes by hand to release the juice and mix in with the olive oil to make a tomato liquid dressing. Allow to sit in the refrigerator for approximately 1 hour, turning every 15 minutes to allow flavour to seep into tomato.

   Place into a large salad bowl. Top with Pane Duro, which has been lightly moistened with water and sprinkled with olive oil, oregano and salt.

Cauolo di Fiori

CAULIFLOWER FRITTERS

PREPARATION TIME: *30* MINUTES
COOKING TIME: *7* MINUTES
SERVES: *4*

1 large cauliflower, cut into florets
salt and pepper
¼ cup milk
2 eggs

1 cup parmesan cheese
4 cups breadcrumbs
750ml (1½ pints) cottonseed oil for
    shallow frying

In a pot, bring water to the boil and add cauliflower. Cook until tender being careful not to overcook the vegetables. Strain and set aside to completely cool.

In a flat soup bowl, combine parmesan cheese and bread crumbs. Beat the eggs and the milk together into another bowl. Season cauliflower florets, coat with egg wash and dip into the cheese and breadcrumb mix.

Heat oil in a frying pan and deep fry cauliflower until golden brown. Remove from oil and allow to drain on absorbent paper before serving.

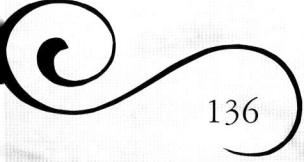 

Everybody should experience the pleasure of eating a fresh fennel salad tossed with olive oil and vinegar. The explosion of taste is indescribable.

Insalata di Finocchi

FENNEL SALAD

PREPARATION TIME: 10 MINUTES

SERVES: 3

1 large fennel bulb

1 punnet (250g/9oz) cherry tomatoes

30ml (1 fl oz) white wine vinegar

4 teaspoons extra virgin olive oil

pinch of salt

Cut the top off the fennel and slice bulb into thin strips. Cut cherry tomatoes into quarters. In a separate bowl mix vinegar, oil and salt. Serve over fennel.

Tip

You can add a handful of baby spinach leaves if liked, but it's a hit all on its own.

Pasta Piselli

PASTA WITH PEAS

PREPARATION TIME: 10 MINUTES

COOKING TIME: 35 MINUTES

SERVES: 4

¼ cup extra virgin olive oil

1 brown onion, diced

1 garlic clove, sliced

2 rashes of pancetta or bacon (optional)

250g (9 oz) pack of peas, frozen

½ cup of water

300ml (10 oz) pureed tomatoes

2 tablespoons white sugar

salt and white pepper, to season

3 fresh basil leaves

1 packet short pasta

parmesan cheese, to serve

In a deep pot, heat the oil then add the onion, garlic and pancetta if using and cook until onion is translucent. Add peas, stir and cover for 3 minutes. Add water and continue to boil, stirring, for 5 minutes. Add tomatoes and boil for a further 5 minutes. Turn down the heat and add sugar and season with salt and pepper.

Simmer on a low heat for a further 20 minutes, adding fresh basil in the final minutes of cooking. Bring another pot of water to the boil and cook pasta until al dente. Reserve some of the water to add to sauce if required.

Serve pasta with sauce on top and finish with a sprinkle of parmesan cheese.

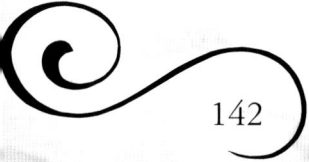

Pasta Fagolini

PASTA WITH ITALIAN BEANS

PREPARATION TIME: 15 MINUTES

COOKING TIME: 45 MINUTES

SERVES: 4

1 packet linguini pasta

1 onion, sliced

1 garlic clove, sliced

1 small piece of veal or beef

1 bay leaf

1 x 400g (14 oz) can diced tomatoes

15 flat Italian (Romano) green beans

1 zucchini/courgette diced

1 potato diced

½ cup of water

In a large pot of boiling water, cook linguini according to packet directions. Meanwhile, clean and string beans, then set aside.

Heat oil in a pot and add onion and garlic, cook until onion is translucent. Add veal and bay leaf, and gently brown. Add tomatoes, beans and water and bring to a boil for 5 minutes. Reduce heat and cook for aproximately 25 minutes, until beans are tender. Add zucchini and potato and cook for a further 10 minutes. When pasta is al dente, drain, conserving a cup of the cooking water. Remove bay leaf from sauce, adding water if required. Stir bean sauce through pasta until heated through and serve.

Tip
Linguini is a nice complement to this dish. Long, flat and lean just like the beans.

In this, like most traditional Italian dishes, the colours of the flag should all be proudly represented – red (carrots), white (bechamel sauce) and green (peas).

Pasta al Forno

PASTA BAKE

PREPARATION TIME: *40 MINUTES*

COOKING TIME: *1 HOUR*

SERVES: *4*

150g (5¼ oz) macaroni pasta, cooked

200ml (7 fl oz) extra virgin olive oil, plus
   1 tablespoon extra oil

3 medium eggplant/aubergine, sliced
   thinly

1 tablespoon butter

60g (2 oz) breadcrumbs

500g (1lb) bolognaise ragú
   (see Basic Recipes)

100g (3½ oz) grated parmesan cheese

80g (3 oz) ham, diced into cubes

80g (3 oz) baby peas, cooked

150ml (5 fl oz) béchamel sauce
   (see Basic Recipes)

4 eggs, hard boiled

Napolitana Sauce (see Basic Recipes)

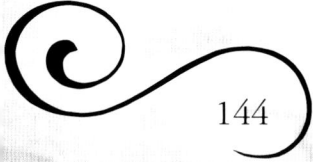

Preheat oven to 180°C/350°F. In a large bowl, toss cooked and lightly cooled macaroni in 1 tablespoon of olive oil. Heat olive oil in a pan and fry sliced aubergine until golden on each side. Set aside on absorbent paper to cool.

Line 4 large ramekins with butter and breadcrumbs and layer each with fried aubergine, allowing it to go over the edge of the ramekin to fold over once assembled. Combine bolognaise sauce, ½ of the parmesan cheese, macaroni, diced ham, peas, and béchamel, stirring gently so as not to mix in bechamel sauce completely.

Place bolognaise mixture in ramekins until a quarter filled. Place a boiled egg in the centre, then fill ramekin with remaining mixture. Fold over eggplant to make a cover and bake for 20-25 minutes. Add remaining parmesan cheese to serve.

Served with thick Napolitana sauce (see Basic Recipes).

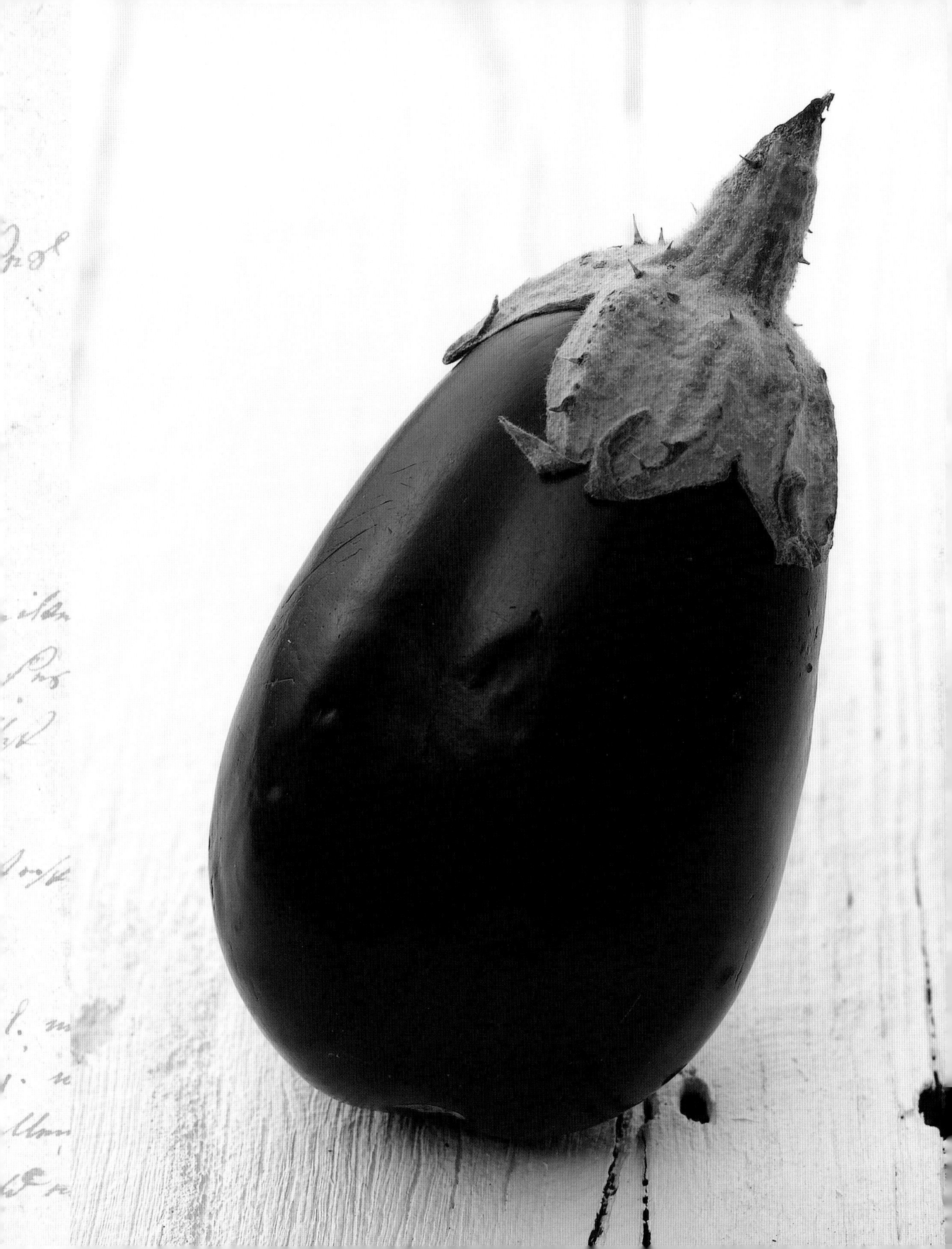

Nonno would eat this almost every day, alternating it with Pasta Ceci. Nonno used to say it was why he had no punsa (stomach).
He was a lean man!

Pasta Fagioli

PASTA WITH CANNELLINI BEANS

PREPARATION TIME: **30** MINUTES

COOKING TIME: **1½** HOURS

SERVES: **4**

500g (1lb) cannellini beans, dried

2 cups water

¼ cup olive oil

2 garlic cloves

2 sage leaves

1 fresh chilli, chopped

3 peeled tomatoes

salt and pepper

200g (7oz) macaroni pasta

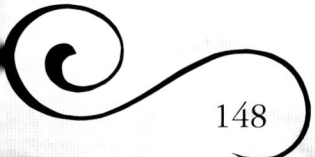

Bring beans to the boil in a pan of lightly salted water and cook until just tender, about an hour.

Once the beans are three-quarters done, set aside, retaining cooking broth. Heat olive oil in a deep pot over a medium heat. When oil is hot, add garlic, chilli and the sage. Cook until the sage is crisp and the garlic is lightly browned. Add the tomatoes and cook for a few more minutes, then add the beans and half a cup of bean cooking broth to cover. Season with salt and pepper, and simmer until the beans are quite soft, stirring occasionally and adding bean broth as necessary to keep bean mixture from drying out.

Boil pasta, reserving some of the water after the pasta has cooked to add to the beans if necessary. Place in a bowl and drizzle with quality extra virgin olive oil to serve.

Tip

You can add Italian pork sausages to the pot after the garlic has been added, sliced thickly, for a more hearty meal.

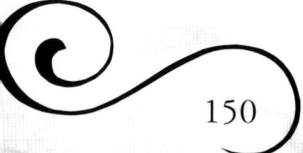

Filetto di Manzo con Salmoriglio

BEEF FILLET WITH OLIVE OIL, LEMON, HERB AND GARLIC SAUCE

PREPARATION TIME: 3 HOURS

COOKING TIME: 25 MINUTES

SERVES: 4

80ml (2 ²/₃ fl oz) olive oil,
  plus 40ml extra
4 x 280g (10 oz) eye fillet steak
salt and pepper

SAUCE/SALMORIGLIO

1 bunch parsley, finely chopped
2 sprigs rosemary
½ bunch thyme
¼ bunch oregano
1 birdseye chilli, split in half
2 garlic cloves, crushed
¼ lemon, juiced
250ml (8½ fl oz) extra virgin olive oil
salt and pepper
2 lemons, halved
sea salt

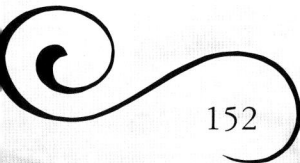

Preheat oven to 220°C/430°F. To make sauce, strip all leaves from herbs and discard the stems. Finely chop herbs and place into a bowl. Add split chilli, crushed garlic cloves, lemon juice and a tablespoon of olive oil. Season herb mixture with salt and pepper and set aside.

Bring fillets to room temperature, season and sprinkle with a tablespoon of olive oil. Heat pan to smoking, add remaining olive oil and sear fillets for 3 minutes each side for approximately 1½ minutes to seal the sides, until the fillet is completely sealed.

Remove from pan and place on a heatproof tray in a preheated oven for approximately 8 minutes. Remove fillet from oven and allow to rest for 7 minutes.

Once rested, place fillet back into oven and reheat for 2 minutes. Place fillets on a serving dish and pour over the sauce.

Serve with a lemon wedge and sea salt.

Petto di Pollo al Marsala

CHICKEN BREASTS WITH MARSALA

PREPARATION TIME: 15 MINUTES

COOKING TIME: 12 MINUTES

SERVES: 4

4 single skinless chicken thigh or breast
  on the bone
salt and pepper
100g (3½ oz) plain flour
  (all-purpose flour)
60ml (2 fl oz) extra virgin olive oil

1 garlic clove, thinly sliced
120ml (4 fl oz) marsala
4 bay leaves
60ml (2 fl oz) thickened cream
30g (1oz) unsalted butter

Season each piece of chicken and dust with flour. In a pan, heat garlic and oil and add chicken and lightly fry until golden on both sides. Add marsala and bay leaves and simmer for 1-2 minutes. Add cream and butter and reduce until sauce thickens. Season to taste.

Pollo al Bianco

CHICKEN IN WHITE WINE

PREPARATION TIME: 15 MINUTES

COOKING TIME: 45 MINUTES

SERVES: 4

1 x 1½kg (3lb) chicken, cut into 8 pieces
120g (4 oz) plain flour
   (all-purpose flour)
salt and pepper
100ml (3½ fl oz) extra virgin olive oil
5 garlic cloves, crushed

1 sprig rosemary
100ml (3½ fl oz) white wine
5 medium potatoes, peeled and cubed
½ teaspoon dried oregano
salt

Coat chicken pieces in seasoned flour. In a heavy–based pot add oil and heat until it starts to smoke.

Carefully add chicken pieces and fry until golden brown all over. Add garlic and half of the rosemary, and colour slightly, then add white wine to stop the garlic from burning. Add potato, oregano and remaining rosemary, season with salt to taste.

Cover and allow to cook for 30 minutes, stirring from time to time to prevent chicken from sticking to the the base of the pot.

Enjoy with freshly baked bread.

Vitello Cotoletta

VEAL SCHNITZEL

PREPARATION TIME: **10** MINUTES

COOKING TIME: **10** MINUTES

SERVES: 4

salt and pepper

6 veal steaks, pounded thinly

3 eggs

120ml (4fl oz) milk

1½ cups breadcrumbs

½ cup parmesan cheese

¼ cup finely chopped parsley

olive oil for frying

Lightly beat the veal with a mallet and season both sides. In a bowl, mix eggs and milk together. In another bowl, combine breadcrumbs, parmesan cheese and parsley. Dip veal into egg mixture, then into the crumb mixture, coating both sides evenly.

In a frying pan add a generous amount of olive oil and fry veal on both sides for 3 minutes each side until lightly golden. Remove from pan and allow to drain on paper towels before serving.

Tip

You may also use chicken or pork. For a crusty, elevated crumb coat veal in plain flour first (before egg mix) then proceed with other steps. This will give you a crumb that rises off your meat.

Vitello Spezatino

VEAL STEW

PREPARATION TIME: 20 MINUTES

COOKING TIME: 1 HOUR

SERVES: 2

extra virgin olive oil

1 onion, sliced

1 birdseye chilli, chopped

500g (1lb) veal chops

5 plump tomatoes or 1 x 400g (14oz)
  can diced tomatoes

3 potatoes cut into wedges

¼ cup water

freshly cracked pepper and salt

Heat oil in a deep pot and fry onion and chilli. Add veal and lightly brown, then add tomatoes and seasoning. Reduce heat to a simmer. Add potatoes and combine well, pour in water and stir thoroughly. Cover and simmer for 45 minutes, stirring occassionally.

Tip
Be careful not to overcook the potatoes or they will end up mashed.

Torta di Ricotta

RICOTTA CHEESECAKE

PREPARATION TIME: 45 MINUTES

COOKING TIME: 50 MINUTES

SERVES: 10

500g (1lb) shortbread pastry
1kg (2lbs) ricotta
350g (12¹/₃ oz) icing sugar
100ml (3½ fl oz) thickened cream

250g (9 oz) mascarpone
2 tablespoons vanilla essence
40g icing sugar, to dust

Preheat oven to 190°C/375°F. Roll out pastry to 3mm (one-eighth of an inch) thick, leaving enough aside to form a top for the cake. Line a 25cm (10 ins) round sponge mould pan with canola spray and place pastry inside pan, pushing gently into corners of the pan.

Dust inside pastry case with cinnamon. In a bowl, whisk ricotta, icing sugar, thickened cream, mascarpone and vanilla essence together until smooth. Pour ricotta mixture into the pastry crust and roll out remaining pastry to top cake. Pinch pastry edges together and crimp with a fork. Bake for 30 minutes. Remove from oven and allow to cool in the pan. Before serving, dust with icing sugar. Use a wire rack to create shapes on the top.

Pastini Mandorlatti

PISTACHIO BISCUITS

PREPARATION TIME: 10 MINUTES

SET ASIDE TIME: 18 HOURS

MAKES: 40 BISCUITS

330g (1 oz) pistachios

600g (1¹/₃ lbs) caster sugar (superfine sugar)

12 egg whites

35g (1¼ oz) glucose

½ tablespoon Super Montigo (or rum)

½ tablespoon Lacrime (or Italian liqueur like Sambucca)

400g (14oz) flaked almond

½ tablespoon Strega essence (Italian liqueur)

160g (2oz) pure icing sugar

1 teaspoon vanilla essence

Place shelled pistachios, sugar and egg whites into a mortar and pestle and grind into a paste. Place the pistachio paste into a mixing bowl and beat with the remaining ingredients until it starts to stick to the side of the mixing bowl.

Once ready, pipe teardrop shaped pieces onto greaseproof paper on a baking tray, cover and set aside for 18 hours.

Preheat oven to 180°C/350°F and bake for 7 minutes.

Sometimes we would arrive home from school to see a chocolate cake or biscotti on the kitchen bench, and I just knew that Zia (Aunty) had paid a visit. Zia Vittoria always added the finishing touches to everything she did, especially cooking.

Zia Vittoria's Limone & Mandorle Biscotti

Aunt Vittoria's lemon and almond biscuits

Preparation time: 30 minutes, plus chilling

Cooking time: 40 minutes

Makes: 30 - 40

250g (9 oz) unsalted butter

¾ cup castor sugar

3 eggs

2 tablespoons rum

2 tablespoons grated lemon rind

2 teaspoons grated lemon essence

170g (6oz) plain flour (all-purpose flour), sifted

150g (5oz) self-raising flour, sifted

¼ teaspoon salt

180g (3 oz) slivered almonds

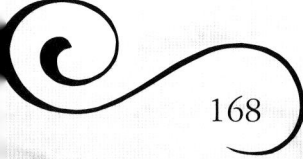

Heat oven to 180°C/350°F. Line two large baking trays with baking paper. In a large bowl, cream the butter and sugar, then add eggs one at a time. Add rum, lemon rind and lemon essence, mix well. Fold the sifted flours and salt into the butter mixture and stir well. Finally, stir in the toasted almonds. Refrigerate for approximately 1 hour.

Remove from fridge, and shape the dough into logs (6 to 8 logs) and place 2 or 3 on each tray. Bake for approximately 20 minutes or until golden brown, but not fully cooked through. Remove from the oven and cool. Using a serrated knife, cut the cooked dough logs on an angle into 1-2cm ($^1/_3$ to $^2/_3$ thirds of an inch) rounds.

Place biscuits back onto the trays, soft side up, and bake for an additional 20 minutes, or until biscuits are dry and crunchy.

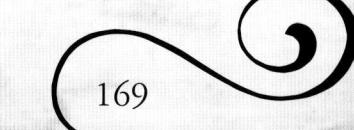

Winter

Breakfast

Coffee with egg

Starter

*Fried rice balls with bolognaise
  and cheese*

Spicy Calabrese soft salami

Lentil soup

Minestrone soup

Chicken soup

Stuffed artichokes

Side

Aunt Tomasina's potato cakes

Leaf salad

Chickpea and pancetta stew

*Spinach with breadcrumbs
  and parmesan*

Peppers in oil

Fried potato cakes

Pasta

*Pasta with artichokes
  and broad beans*

Linguine with broccoli

Pumpkin and sage tortellini

Main Course

*Rabbit stew with tomato
  and basil*

Meatballs

Braised chilli ribs

*Veal rolls stuffed with eggs,
  cheese and herbs*

Sweet

Mini chocolate pudding

Trifle

Papá's Produce

Papá would go to the ends of the earth to find quality produce. He would regularly hand-pick his grapes to make his wine. Papá always made reference to the importance of the good, rich quality of the soil. The climate was paramount too, and Papá knew that his wine, with it's hand selected grapes, along with the traditions of his secret recipe, would result in a beautiful product.

Cosimo's Wine.

Ma tells us stories of Papá sneaking away to the cellar – an underground concrete basement that stunk of vinegared eggplant, earthy potatoes, and preserved olives and sundried tomato – and watching the wine ferment. He'd get a heater and place it in front of the wine barrels to hasten the process, much to Ma's frustration. The way Papá cared for that wine was so telling of the way he treated all food processes – with care and attention. Food to him was sacred, and this legacy has been passed down to our family.

Papá Cosimo gives a speech on his wedding day.

For large family gatherings, relatives would be invited by a quick phone call; invitations were rarely ever sent out because verbal invitations were always honoured, unless it was a wedding or a christening. If it was a holy event, like Christmas or Easter, everyone would go to church first, except the men who'd always stay home and do last minute food preparations or play cards. When everyone returned from mass, the whole family would unite for the official family photos and then the buffet lunch would begin. The celebrations were always centred around the table, which was big enough for us all.

The Celebration Table

The men assumed the heads of the table, and it was when they sat down that everyone began to eat. The kids were generally fed first and then the adults began to eat, except the women, including Ma and Nonna, who were always in the kitchen and ate last as they had to make sure that everyone had a plate. Again, if you were eating, you were being looked after and cared for. The table groaned under the weight of lasagne, spaghetti, veal schnitzels, zucchini flowers, zupoli, olives, antipasto, wine, beans, spinach meatballs – and on it went. We would settle down to fruit after the huge meal, then an amazing variety of dessert selections: tiramisu, gelato, cannoli, ricotta cake, profiteroles, biscotti, gelato and finally, a shot of espresso or two. The men, while enjoying an affogato, would play a game of cards and it was the yelling and banter and the not-so-serious arguments about who had the winning hand that marked the end of a very indulgent day with la famiglia.

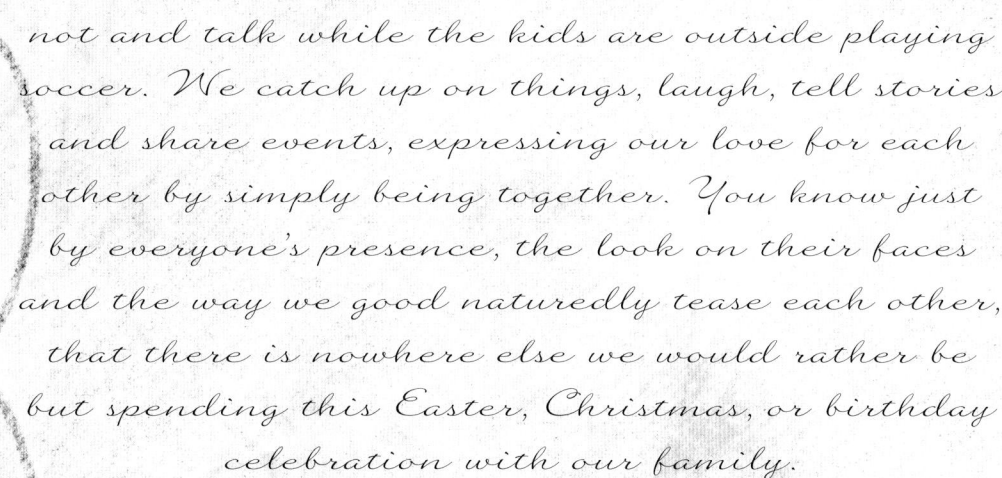

Although we have since grown-up and started families of our own, we still gather at Ma and Papa's house for celebrations, which are now made even more chaotic with the addition of grandchildren. We still always sit around the table whether we were eating or not and talk while the kids are outside playing soccer. We catch up on things, laugh, tell stories and share events, expressing our love for each other by simply being together. You know just by everyone's presence, the look on their faces and the way we good naturedly tease each other, that there is nowhere else we would rather be but spending this Easter, Christmas, or birthday celebration with our family.

We would wake up in the winter mornings to a home already warm and the smell of fresh coffee filling the house. But our coffee was special, on these winter mornings my father was convinced that we needed protein as well as a hit of espresso to commence the day, wake us up and keeps us warm. Ma would give us bread to dip into the coffee too.

Cafe con Uovo

COFFEE WITH EGG

COOKING TIME: 5 MINUTES

SERVES: 1

1 shot of espresso
200ml (7 fl oz) warmed milk

1 teaspoon of sugar
1 egg yolk

Prepare a shot of espresso and heat the milk on a stovetop. In a mug, place sugar and one egg yolk, and whisk briskly for at least 2 minutes, until frothy. Add the espresso and whisk again for a further minute. Tilting your mug on an angle, gradually add your hot milk before enjoying.

Tip
Add a teaspoon of cocoa with the sugar for mocha.

Arancino di Riso

FRIED RICE BALLS WITH BOLOGNAISE AND CHEESE

PREPARATION TIME: 3½ HOURS

COOKING TIME: 1 HOUR 45 MINUTES

SERVES: 4

160ml (2 fl oz) extra virgin olive oil

1 medium brown onion, finely chopped

pinch saffron

480g (17 oz) Arborio (risotto) rice

800g (28 oz) chicken stock

260g (9 oz) grated parmesan cheese

120g (4 oz) unsalted butter

200g (7 oz) bolognaise ragú (see Basics chapter)

40g (1½ oz) peas, cooked

40g (1½ oz) Italian soft cheese, such as provolone or mozzarella, grated

4 eggs

60ml (2 fl oz) milk

200g (7 oz) plain flour (all-purpose flour)

350g (12¹/₃ oz) breadcrumbs

2L (4 pints) cottonseed oil

salt

In a heavy based pot heat olive oil and fry onion and saffron. Add rice and cook for a further 4 minutes.

Heat chicken stock and pour slowly into rice until all liquid has been absorbed, stirring continually. Add grated parmesan cheese and butter and stir well. Remove from heat and allow to cool until all liquid has absorbed.

Meanwhile, in a bowl, mix bolognaise ragú and cooked peas. Once rice mixture has cooled, place a dessertspoon of mixture in the palm of your hand, approximately 1cm (¹/₃ ins) thick. Fill centre with bolognaise and pea mixture, add a sprinkle of cheese and cover with a little more rice mixture. Shape into a cone between two sheets of cling film, ensuring all edged are sealed and place in refrigerator for 3 hours.

In a bowl, beat eggs and milk together. Once rice balls have set, roll in flour then into beaten egg and milk, then in breadcrumb. Repeat the egg and crumb for each ball, until all have a double coating. To cook, deep fry in hot oil until golden brown.

Nduja

SPICY CALABRESE SOFT SALAMI

PREPARATION TIME: 2 HOURS PLUS 4 WEEKS CURING

MAKES: 1KG (2LB) SALAMI

1kg (2l bs) good quality pork mince paste
30g (1 oz) salt
50g (1¾ oz) chilli powder

50g (1¾ oz) chilli paste
1 large sausage skin
1 metre (3¼ feet) butchers' string

Place pork mince paste on a marble or stainless steel table and sprinkle with salt, chilli powder and chilli paste. Bring to room temperature and mix by hand, making sure to thoroughly incorporate all the ingredients. Squash mince in between fingers to mix in chilli. Rest for 30 minutes.

Tie the end of the salami skin with butchers' string, fill sausage skin with meat mixture and pack tightly by twisting the top of the sausage skin until the meat is tight packed at the bottom. Repeat until salami is approximately 20cm (8 ins) long. Twist and tie off with remaining butchers' string. Hang in a cool dry wine cellar or store at a constant temperature of 9-16°C (48-60°F) for a minimum of 4 weeks until salami has fully cured.

It was in Nonno's garage that an annual ritual took place: the making of the salami. This would be done in winter so the salami would last us through the year. It was an enjoyable process as the extended family would come together and have a great big barbecue while churning, stuffing, tying, and pricking the salami. The smell of lemon-soaked intestines is still with me. There was always a beautiful conversation around the table followed by the discussion about who had placed an order but was a no-show to help! Papà really shined through the whole process giving everyone tips and advice on how they should be doing things. Zio Frank would put some of the fresh pork meat onto a little barbecue, and then onto an Italian panini (bread) roll. Papà operated the machine, with Nonno standing on the opposite end with the intestines waiting to be filled. Papà thought that Nonno didn't prick the salami enough and so recruited us over-zealous kids to also prick the stuffed-intestines – a procedure that we didn't really understand at the time. We just thought it was a pretend job that we'd been given by the grown-ups to keep us interested.

*Lentils are a New Years Day tradition in Italy.
They resemble coins and so they are believed to
bring good luck and prosperity.*

Zuppa di Lenticchie

LENTIL SOUP

PREPARATION TIME: 30 MINUTES

COOKING TIME: 2 HOURS

SERVES: 8

¼ cup olive oil

1 large onion, chopped

1 large carrot, chopped

2 celery stalks, chopped

1 x 200g (7 oz) canned diced tomatoes

500g (1 lb) lentils, rinsed

1½ cups chopped spinach

½ cup fresh peas

12 cups of water

20g (¾oz) butter

salt and pepper

50g (1¾oz) grated parmesan cheese

Pane di casa or crusty bread

Heat oil in a pan, add chopped onion, carrot and celery and heat through for 5 minutes. Add diced tomatoes and simmer for 5 minutes. Add lentils and peas stirring continuously to coat the lentils for a few minutes. Add water then simmer on a low to medium heat for 20 minutes. Reduce heat to low for 1 ½ hours. Add spinach, butter and seasoning. Sprinkle with parmesan cheese to taste and serve with crusty bread. Soup will keep for up to 6 months in freezer.

Tip

French or green lentils hold their shape and have a lovely flavour. If liked, add cauliflower florets with spinach.

Minestrone

MINESTRONE SOUP

PREPARATION TIME: *30 MINUTES*

COOKING TIME: *2½ HOURS*

SERVES: *8*

2 onions, chopped

2 carrots, chopped

3 celery stalks, chopped

2 zucchini (courgettes), chopped

1 large sweet potato, chopped

¾ cup peas

¾ cup beans, chopped into 3cm
  (1 in) pieces

¼ cup extra virgin olive oil

1 x 400g (14 oz) can of cannellini
  (white) beans

1 x 400g (14oz) can diced tomatoes

20g (¾ oz) butter

salt and pepper

4L (8 pints) water

parmesan cheese, to serve

Chop all vegetables and set aside. Heat oil in a large pot and saute onions, then add vegetables and coat evenly in oil. Add tomatoes, season with salt and pepper and coat once again. Add cannellini beans and water and bring to a boil for 10 minutes, then simmer for 2 hours. Add butter in the last 30 minutes of cooking. Serve with parmesan cheese grated on top.

Tip

You can also add a range of vegetables, such as potatoes and cabbage. Minestrone will keep for 10 days in the fridge and freezes well.

Brodo alla Pollo

CHICKEN SOUP

PREPARATION TIME: 30 MINUTES

COOKING TIME: 2 HOURS

SERVES: 6

2L (64fl oz) water

4 chicken drumsticks, skin removed

4 celery stalks, chopped

4 carrots, chopped

2 small potatoes, diced

1 whole brown onion, chopped

¼ cup tomato purée

1 tablespoon salt

1 bunch parsley, chopped

CHICKEN BALLS

150g (5¼ oz) chicken mince

1 egg

½ cup breadcrumbs

½ cup parmesan cheese

salt

To make the broth, fill a pot with water and bring to the boil. Rinse the chicken drumsticks and add to the pot. Cook over a medium heat. Then add celery, carrots, potatoes, onion, tomato purée and salt.

Bring to the boil, reduce heat and simmer for 2 hours. At the end of cooking, discard the onion, remove drumsticks, shred chicken and place back into pot, discarding bones. Add parsley.

For the chicken balls, place chicken mince in a large bowl and add remaining parsley, egg, breadcrumbs, parmesan cheese and salt to taste. Roll into thumbnail size balls. Add to pot when simmering so they don't break up. Simmer for 20 minutes until the chicken is cooked.

Carciofi Ripiene

STUFFED ARTICHOKES

PREPARATION TIME: 30 MINUTES

COOKING TIME: 55 MINUTES

SERVES: 4

8 medium sized artichokes

100g (3½ oz) plain flour
(all-purpose flour)

60ml (2 fl oz) lemon juice

4L (8 pints) water

120g (4 oz) double smoked ham, cut
into small dice

2 garlic cloves, chopped

½ birdseye chilli, finely sliced

200g (7 oz) parmesan cheese, grated,

100g (3½ oz) breadcrumbs

salt and pepper

¼ bunch parsley, finely chopped

8 basil leaves, finely chopped

Heat oven to 200°C/390°F. Cut the tops off the artichokes and peel off the exterior leaves to reveal the inner yellow leaf. Trim stalk, retaining any of the usable meat from the stalk for the filling. To stop artichokes going brown, mix flour, lemon juice and three quarters of the water in a large bowl. Place artichokes in bowl with flour and water mix.

In a food processor add ham, garlic, chilli, parmesan cheese, breadcrumbs, salt and pepper. Process till combined, then add chopped parsley and sliced basil. Mix well. Remove artichoke leaves from flour and water mixture and drain. Place breadcrumb mixture between leaves, making sure to pack tightly. Place stuffed leaves in a heavy based pan and top with breadcrumb and grated parmesan cheese mixture. Pour over remaining water and place pan in oven until cheese and breadcrumbs are golden in colour, about 20 minutes.

Zia (Aunt) Tomasina is Papá's older sister. She recently passed away but this was her signature dish. She made it for all the family functions.

Tomasina's Gatto di Patate

AUNT TOMASINA'S POTATO CAKES

PREPARATION TIME: *45 MINUTES*

COOKING TIME: *1 HOUR*

SERVES: *6*

1kg (2lbs) potatoes, peeled

50g (1¾ oz) parmesan cheese, grated, plus 30g (1 oz) extra for garnish

2 eggs

¼ teaspoon nutmeg

100g (3½ oz) soft Italian cheese, such as mozzarella

120g (4oz) ham, cut into small dice

100g (3½ oz) soft cheese ,such as scamorza, cut into small dice

salt and pepper

Preheat oven to 180°C/350°F. In a large pan, boil potatoes until fully cooked and mash while hot. Add mashed potato to a large bowl with parmesan cheese, egg and nutmeg, and mix well. Once combined, add mozzarella, ham, scamorza, salt and pepper to taste.

Place in a ceramic baking tray and sprinkle with parmesan cheese, then bake until parmesan is golden brown and potato cake is hot in the centre. Serve as a side, best with a drizzle of truffle oil.

Insalata Lascia

LEAF SALAD

PREPARATION TIME: *10 MINUTES*
COOKING TIME: *15 MINUTES*
SERVES: *4*

800g (1¾lbs) rape leaves
  (or turnip tops)
4 garlic cloves, chopped

150ml (5 fl oz) olive oil
salt
50g (1¾ oz) cannelini beans

Rinse leaves. Bring a pot of salted water to the boil, cook rape leaves for 12 to 14 minutes until tender but still with a slight crunch. Remove leaves from water and place in a salad bowl. Allow to cool. Season with finely chopped garlic, olive oil and some salt. Mix with cannellini beans and serve.

Tip
Rape leaf is available from good Italian green grocers. If unavailable, use the green tops of turnips.

Ceci e Pancetta

CHICKPEA (GARBANZO BEANS) AND PANCETTA STEW

PREPARATION TIME: 20 MINUTES

COOKING TIME: 55 MINUTES

SERVES: 10

80ml (2 ²/₃ fl oz) extra virgin olive oil

250g (9 oz) pancetta

4 garlic cloves, thinly sliced

2 birdseye chillies, thinly sliced

1 medium brown onion, finely diced

3 x 420g (14¾oz) cans of chickpeas
   (garbanzo beans)

500ml (1 pint) chicken stock

100g (3½ oz) parmesan cheese, grated

40g (1½ oz) unsalted butter

½ bunch parsley, finely chopped

salt and pepper

In a heavy-based pot add olive oil, pancetta, thinly sliced garlic, chilli and onion and saute until garlic starts to colour but not brown.

Drain chickpeas and add to pot with chicken stock and slightly mash some of the chickpeas. Cook for approximately 15 minutes on a medium heat.

Take off the heat and immediately add parmesan cheese, butter, parsley, salt and pepper. Stir thoroughly and serve.

Spinaci Parmigiano Reggiano

SPINACH WITH BREADCRUMBS AND PARMESAN

PREPARATION TIME: 30 MINUTES

COOKING TIME: 2½ HOURS

SERVES: 4

1 bunch spinach, chopped	1 cup parmesan cheese
¹/₃ cup extra virgin olive oil	½ cup breadcrumbs
2 garlic cloves, sliced	salt to season

Cut and rinse spinach well, remove most of the stalk and discard. Bring a large pot of water to the boil, add the spinach and cook for 20 minutes, strain and set aside. In a pot, heat the oil and add the garlic, stirring, until a nice garlic scent has been released.

Add the spinach to the pot with the garlic, add parmesan cheese, breadcrumbs and salt, stirring on a medium heat until the spinach is coated, then serve.

Tip
This dish is a great side to any winter meal, and can be also be created using endive.

Pepperonata

PEPPERS IN OIL

PREPARATION TIME: *15 MINUTES*

COOKING TIME: *12 MINUTES*

SERVES: *4*

120ml (4fl oz) extra virgin olive oil

2 large red capsicum/bell peppers, cut into finger-sized pieces

2 large yellow capsicum/bell peppers, cut into finger-sized pieces

2 large green capsicum/bell peppers, cut into finger-sized pieces

4 garlic cloves, crushed with a knife

4 birdseye chillies, sliced

2 medium potatoes, cut into fingers

1 punnet (250g/9 oz) cherry tomatoes

salt and pepper

12 basil leaves

parsley to garnish

Heat a large fry pan until it starts to smoke. Add extra virgin olive oil and potato and fry until it starts to turn golden. Add capsicum, garlic, chilli, basil and halved cherry tomatoes and fry until they all become soft.

Finish with salt and pepper and parsley.

Tip
A Crinitis' speciality is to add veal strips after the potato.

Croche di Patate

FRIED POTATO CAKES

PREPARATION TIME: *30* MINUTES

COOKING TIME: *20* MINUTES

SERVES: *10*

1kg (2lbs) desiree potatoes, diced

1½ cups plain flour (all-purpose flour)

1 egg yolk

50g (1¾ oz) butter

½ cup parmesan cheese

¼ teaspoons salt

2L (4 pints) cottonseed oil for deep frying

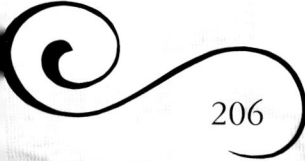

Bring a pot of water to the boil, add the potatoes and cook until soft. Drain the water and mash the potatoes well. Allow potatoes to cool for 30 minutes, then add half the flour, egg yolk, butter and parmesan cheese, combine well (this is best done with your hands). Add the remainder of the flour until a soft but not sticky consistency is reached. The amount of flour required will depend on the consistency of the potatoes, so feeling the dough with your hands will help to achieve the right texture for the dough.

Taking small handfuls of the dough, shape into balls and roll in flour so the cakes do not disintegrate when frying. Heat oil in a frying pan and deep fry the croche's until golden. Remove from oil, place onto absorbent paper, sprinkle with salt, then serve.

Tip

Mash potatoes while hot and then allow to completely cool before making into a dough, otherwise the potato may go lumpy.

Pasta Carciofi e Fave

PASTA WITH ARTICHOKES AND BROAD BEANS

PREPARATION TIME: 25 MINUTES

COOKING TIME: 25 MINUTES

SERVES: 4

125ml (4fl oz) cup extra virgin olive oil
2 garlic cloves, sliced
1 brown onion, sliced
1 lemon, juiced
12 baby artichokes

300g (10 oz) broad beans, peeled
750g (1½ lb) tagliatelle
½ cup parsley, chopped
salt and pepper

In a cold pan heat olive oil, garlic and onion until the garlic starts to colour. Add lemon juice, artichokes and broad beans and combine until well coated with oil, garlic and onion.

Meanwhile, bring a large pan of salted water to the boil and cook pasta until al dente, according to packet directions. Drain cooked pasta, reserving one cup of pasta water, and add pasta to pan, stirring to combine well. Add parsley and pasta water to your taste. Season to taste.

Tip

If pasta is a little dry after all ingredients are combined, gradually add small amounts of reserved water from pasta and an extra drizzle of olive oil.

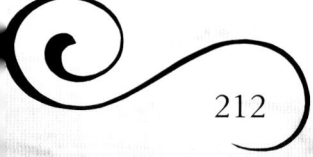

Linguine con Brocoli

LINGUINE WITH BROCCOLI

PREPARATION TIME: 15 MINUTES

COOKING TIME: 15 MINUTES

SERVES: 4

¼ cup pine nuts

125g (4½ oz) pancetta

60ml (2 fl oz) olive oil

4 garlic cloves, minced

1 birdseye chilli, sliced

300g (10 oz) broccoli florets

salt

500g (1lb) linguine

Heat oven to 180°C/350°F. Place pine nuts onto tray and toast in oven for a couple of minutes until golden brown.

In a frying pan cook pancetta with a little oil over a medium heat until crisp, add garlic and chilli. In a large pot of boiling salted water, cook the broccoli until just tender. Add the drained broccoli to the frying pan and stir until combined Bring a large pot of salted water to the boil. Add linguine and cook according to packet directions. Drain and toss with the broccoli, pine nuts and pancetta, season and dress with olive oil to taste.

Tip

To prevent the broccoli from overcooking and breaking up, once drained, place in a bowl of iced water to halt the cooking process.

Tortellini di Zucca e Salvia

PUMPKIN AND SAGE TORTELLINI

PREPARATION TIME: 45 MINUTES

COOKING TIME: 20 MINUTES

SERVES: 6

1kg (2lbs) pumpkin chopped and diced

1 red onion, chopped

200g (7 oz) ricotta cheese

50g (1¾ oz) parmesan cheese

1 egg yolk, plus 1 egg, beaten

nutmeg

salt

¼ cup chopped sage plus 15 leaves

350g (12 ¹/₃ oz) pasta (see Basic Recipes)

120g (4 oz) butter

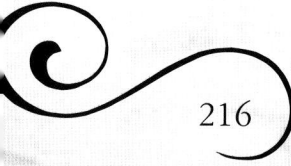

Bring pumpkin and onion to the boil in a pot of salted water. Once cooked, drain. Mash the pumpkin. Discard onion and allow to cool for 10 minutes. Crumble in the ricotta, add the parmesan cheese, egg yolk, nutmeg, salt and sage and combine well. Set to one side and prepare your pasta sheets.

Roll out pasta as thinly as possible, and cut into 5cm (1½ ins) squares. Brush pastry squares with extra egg. Using a teaspoon, add pumpkin filling to the centre of the square and fold on a diagonal to form a triangle, pressing along the edges. Join the two corners and pinch together. Place filled tortellini on baking paper on a baking tray and cover with a tea towel.

Then once they are all made, bring a pan of water to the boil, add the tortellini and cook until al dente, about 6 minutes.

To make the sage butter, simply melt butter in a pan with the sage and allow to infuse for a few minutes, being careful not to burn the butter.

Drizzle on top of the tortellini and serve.

Stufato di Coniglio con Pomodoro e Basilicoi

RABBIT STEW WITH TOMATO AND BASIL

PREPARATION TIME: 35 MINUTES

COOKING TIME: 1 HOUR AND 30 MINUTES

SERVES: 4

100ml (3½ fl oz) extra virgin olive oil

1 rabbit, cut into pieces

1kg (2 lbs) tomatoes, peeled and diced

2 garlic cloves, crushed

1 medium onion, finely diced

10 basil leaves, torn

salt and pepper

Heat oil in a pan and fry rabbit pieces until golden on all sides. Once browned remove from pan, place on a plate, cover and keep warm.

Add onion and garlic to the pan and cook for 2 minutes. Add tomato and ¼ cup of water, and cook over a medium heat for approximately 20 minutes.

Return rabbit to the pan, cover and cook over a medium to low heat for another hour until rabbit is tender. Season with salt and pepper and scatter over basil leaves. Serve with soft polenta or mashed potato.

These meatballs always taste better the next day.

Ma's Polpette

MEATBALLS

PREPARATION TIME: 45 MINUTES

COOKING TIME: 15 MINUTES

MAKES: 10 MEATBALLS

250g (9 oz) breadcrumbs
60ml (2 fl oz) milk
2 eggs
2kg (4 lbs) lean beef mince
4 garlic cloves, minced
½ bunch parsley, chopped
¼ bunch basil, chopped

125g (4½ oz) parmesan cheese, grated
Good grinding of black pepper
15g (½ oz) salt
150g (5¼ oz) plain flour
  (all-purpose flour)
2L (4 pints) vegetable oil

Soak breadcrumbs in milk until soft, strain excess milk. In a large bowl, mix breadcrumbs with eggs, minced beef, garlic, parsley, basil, parmesan cheese, pepper and salt until well combined. Mould into balls of approximately 200g (7oz) size. Roll balls in flour. Heat vegetable oil in a frying pan. Add balls and fry until golden. Best served with Sugo di Pomodoro (see Basic Recipes).

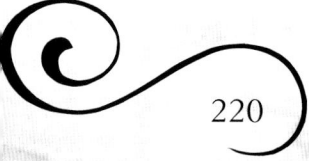

Hunting with Cosimo

In the early mornings Papà and his friends would meet at our place, ready to go on their hunting expeditions.

We would be woken at three in the morning to the smell of the coffee brewing and the sound of all the men's deep whispers downstairs... you could hear the excitement in their voices.

Papà was very adventurous with food. On one occasion, on a hunting trip, he cooked pork ribs in a red sugo and added sausage, salami, pork belly and chilli. It is his sense of adventure that taught us the art of food experimentation from an early age. Here's our version of that recipe.

Costola Brasata con Peperoncino

BRAISED CHILLI RIBS

PREPARATION TIME: 35 MINUTES

COOKING TIME: 2 HOURS, PLUS COOLING

SERVES: 4

500g (1lb) pork baby back ribs

60g (2oz) salt

1.5L (3 pints) water

150ml (5 fl oz) extra virgin olive oil

1 whole fresh chilli, sliced

1 tablespoon dried chilli

1 teaspoon smoked paprika

60g (2oz) Italian pork sausage

60g (2oz) pork chops

60g (2oz) pork belly

60g (2oz) soft cacciatore salami or other
 spicy salami

200ml (7 fl oz) red wine

300ml (10½oz) Napolitana sauce
 (see Basic Recipes)

2 sprigs rosemary

50g (1½oz) cherry tomatoes

pepper

5 basil leaves

Place pork ribs in a pot of salted water and bring to the boil. Reduce heat and simmer for approximately 1 hour and 45 minutes until meat starts to come off the bone. Remove ribs from liquid, discard liquid, and allow ribs to cool completely in refrigerator. In a heavy-based pot add olive oil and heat. Add chilli, paprika, pork sausage, chops, pork belly and salami.

Cook until juices have almost reduced then add red wine and repeat until liquid has reduced and pork starts to colour. Add Napolitana sauce, tomatoes and rosemary. Return ribs to the pot, cook for 15 minutes on medium heat and season to taste. Finish with extra virgin olive oil and torn basil.

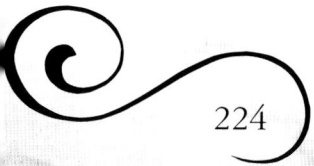

Vitello Arrosto
VEAL ROLLS STUFFED WITH EGGS, CHEESE AND HERBS

PREPARATION TIME: *20 MINUTES*

COOKING TIME: *40 MINUTES*

SERVES: *6*

6 strips prosciutto

6 medium veal steaks, pounded thinly

salt and pepper

½ cup chopped parsley

basil leaves, chopped

¼ cup of fior di latte mozzarella

¼ cup parmesan cheese

4 hard boiled eggs, sliced

string

Heat oven to 180°C/350°F. On a large sheet of cling film, lay the prosciutto strips flat lengthways, slightly overlapping them. Top with veal, seasoned with salt and pepper. Sprinkle parsley and basil down the centre of the meats. Add the cheeses and sliced eggs. Using the cling film to help you, begin rolling along the long side until you have a perfect scroll. Tie rolls with the string.

Remove the rolls from the plastic and brown on all sides in an oiled pan over high heat. Remove from stove and place rolls in the oven for 30 minutes. Remove veal rolls from oven and allow to cool. Remove string and slice to serve.

Chocolate Budino

Mini chocolate pudding

Preparation time: 25 minutes

Cooking Time: 11 minutes

Makes: 10

500g (1lb) cocoa (72 per cent chocolate)

500g (1lb) unsalted butter

20 eggs

500g (1lb) caster sugar (superfine sugar)

500g (1lb) plain flour (all-purpose flour)

Preheat oven to 180°C/350°F. In a stainless steel or glass bowl place chocolate and butter over a double boiler. Melt chocolate and butter, but do not stir. Remove from heat and allow to cool slightly.

Meanwhile, combine eggs and caster sugar and beat until they become white in colour and sugar has completely dissolved. Fold beaten egg into chocolate mixture with flour. Spray dariole or scone moulds with oil spray and pour about 100g (3½ oz) of the mixture into each.

Bake in the oven for about 11 minutes. Remove from oven and allow to sit on the bench for a minute before turning out onto plate. Dust with icing sugar and serve with gelato of your choice.

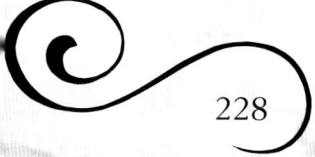

Zuppa Inglese

TRIFLE

PREPARATION TIME: 20 MINUTES

SETTING TIME: 12 HOURS OR OVERNIGHT

SERVES: 12

400g (14oz) vanilla custard
 (see Cannoli recipe)
400g (14oz) chocolate custard
 (see Cannoli recipe)
500ml (16fl oz) Rosso Antico Classic
 Italian Liqueur Syrup

½ lemon zest
½ orange zest
1 x basic vanilla sponge cake (22cm/10in)
 cut into 3 layers approx 3cm (1½in)
 thick (you can buy these at any
 supermarket)
100g (3½oz) icing sugar
fresh cream to serve

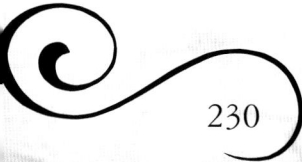

Place a layer of sponge in the base of a tray or glass dish and dampen with Liqueur Syrup. Combine chocolate custard with orange zest. Spread over the syrup soaked sponge.

Place a second layer of sponge in the dish or tray and again dampen with Liqueur Syrup.

Combine vanilla custard with lemon zest and spread over the second layer of sponge.

Finish with third and final layer of custard, dampened with Liqueur Syrup.

Cover the dish with plastic wrap and allow to set in fridge overnight or 12 hours. Dust with icing sugar and serve in slices with fresh cream.

Southern Italian Home Remedies

In our family, food was not only a way to satisfy hunger, but also a way of healing. There were always remedies that utilised the healing properties of food. When we had a cold, Ma would make fresh chicken soup and cover our heads in a towel under a bowl of steaming water and sugar. Before you knew it, the cold was gone; Chamomile was boiled for sore tummies and the tea leaves were put over our eyes to cure conjunctivitis; there was always freshly-squeezed orange juice on the table to ensure we had enough vitamin C.

When one of the little babies was crying and unsettled, Nonna could decipher what the pain was that was causing the little one to be so upset. He has wind, she would say, and heat some olive oil, then massage it in to the belly button in a circular motion before placing a heated towel on the baby's tummy.

The following were some of the things that we
would do at home to treat other minor aliments:
Burns: aloe vera leaves from the garden
Sore tooth: some Grappa
Headache: slice potato, place onto your head and
wrap with a headband
Anxiety: chamomile tea
Cuts: salt in boiled water, allow to cool and apply
to the cut
Stomachache: dry the stems of cherries then boil
and drink the brew when cooled
Worms: loads of extra garlic added to a meal
Sore throat: mix honey and lemon in warm water
and gargle, steeping some sage leaves
in the boiled water
Sinus: salt water inserted into the nose with a
dropper and breathed in was sure to clear our
sinuses

With soccer-mad sons and netballers for daughters, sprains were a common occurrence in our home. Nonna's remedy for sprains is a cold compress wrapped in a cheesecloth over the sprain and changed every two days for a week. Unfortunately, it was also a rather smelly and embarrassing to explain to friends.

half a cup of grated soap
2 tablespoons white vinegar
2 egg whites
half a cup plain flour (all-purpose flour)

Beat the egg whites until frothy then add all ingredients together and mix well until it forms a paste. Then lay the paste on a strip of cheesecloth and apply to the effected area, using a gauze or long bandage. The paste may ooze a little but it will soon harden. Repeat every two days for a week.

Index of recipes

A NOTE ON MEASUREMENTS

1 teaspoon = 5g/5ml
1 tablespoon = 15g/15ml
Liquid measures: 1 cup = 250ml (9fl oz)
Solid measures (vary, depending on substance):
  1 cup caster sugar (superfine sugar) = 220g (8oz);
  1 cup flour = 150g (5oz);
  1 cup white sugar = 225g (24oz)

Oven Temperatures

100°C	very slow	200°F	Gas Mark	1
120°C	very slow	250°F	Gas Mark	1
150°C	slow	300°F	Gas Mark	2
160°C	warm	325°F	Gas Mark	2–3
180°C	moderate	350°F	Gas Mark	4
190°C	moderately hot	375°F	Gas Mark	5
200°C	moderately hot	400°F	Gas Mark	6
220°C	hot	420°F	Gas Mark	7
230°C	very hot	450°F	Gas Mark	8
250°C	very hot	485°F	Gas Mark	9

First published in Australia in 2012 by
New Holland Publishers (Australia) Pty Ltd
London • Sydney • Cape Town • Auckland

86–88 Edgware Road, London W2 2EA United Kingdom
1/66 Gibbes Street, Chatswood NSW 2067 Australia
Wembly Square, First Floor, Solan Road Gardens
  Cape Town 8001 South Africa
218 Lake Road, Northcote Auckland New Zealand

www.newhollandpublishers.com

Publisher: Fiona Schultz
Publishing Director: Lliane Clarke
Designers: Tracy Loughlin
Editor: Bronwyn Phillips
Proofreader: Michele Perry
Food Photographs: Graeme Gillies
Production Director: Olga Dementiev
Printer: Toppan Leefung Printing Ltd (China)

10 9 8 7 6 5 4 3 2 1

A record of this book is held at the British Library and National
  Library of Australia

ISBN 9781742572659

Keep up with New Holland Publishers on Facebook
  http://www.facebook.com/NewHollandPublishers